CH00408893

Warning/Disclaimer

All physical activity comes with an inherent risk, but even more so when using an environment as unpredictable as the outdoors. The information presented within this book is done so with good intentions. You must always consult a qualified physician before embarking on any programme of physical training. Do not take risks that are beyond your current physical capabilities or current fitness levels. You must take full responsibility for your safety and know your limits. This publication is intended for informational use only and I will not assume any liability or be held responsible for any form of injury by the utilisation of this information.

Credit to Kate Shaw for the front cover design and editing the second edition

Preface to the 2nd edition

This second edition of the Woodland Warrior has some grammatical corrections many of which slipped through my clearly uncritical and uneducated net in the first edition. I was in a rush because I wanted to capitalise on the closure of gyms across the UK and globally. It also contains some updated photos of exercise demonstrations.

Why no one left a review mentioning the fact that I'm wearing a horrific combination of leggings and a backwards baseball cap in the first edition is astounding, you should be ashamed of yourselves.

About the Author

Henry grew up on a farm in rural Somerset, England. He developed a passion for strength at a young age, often challenging himself to see how many hay bales he could carry at once.

This passion for strength was only rivalled by his passion for the outdoors. He spent hours exploring nature and being in awe of its complexity.

Henry has competed in both powerlifting and strongman events. In 2019 he established Dagger Camping and Outdoor Pursuits based at Dagger Wood Campsite where he offers wild camping and outdoor activities like foraging workshops, clay pigeon shooting, and Woodland Warrior bootcamps.

To immerse yourself in the Woodland Warrior method, join the author Henry at a Woodland Warrior Bootcamp at Dagger Wood Campsite.

For more information head to www.daggerwoodcampsite.co.uk or the Instagram page @daggerwood_campsite.

You can also order more copies of the Woodland Warrior from the above website or head to our eBay store where you can pick up a Woodland Warrior or Dagger Wood Campsite t-shirt.

Contents

Introduction

As I sit down to begin writing The Woodland Warrior, it's currently the 12th May 2020. I'm outside in rural Somerset enjoying the spring sunshine with a slight breeze every so often touching the back of my neck. The U.K. has been in lockdown for over 7 weeks due to the Coronavirus. While life hasn't changed too dramatically for some, it certainly lacks the 'normality' that many took for granted prior to the pandemic.

I realise my situation is probably an ideal one to be in considering I have access to vast amounts of countryside. Whereas for many life has most likely at times felt unbearable in the confines of their four walls with nothing but rising behemoths of concrete and steel surrounding them.

During this time all gyms, big and small, have been closed completely. As the supervisor of a local gym in a large leisure centre, this has granted me an unusual amount of free time. And for someone who can count on one hand the number of workouts he has missed when it comes to various styles of strength training, it has been strange to not hear the clash of iron upon iron on a daily basis.

For those like me who were lucky enough to have invested in home equipment many moons before this pandemic, we are fortunate to be able to maintain some kind of training programme even with a just a barbell and a few plates.

For a lot of people, the opposite is true. As they anxiously type 'home gym equipment' in any search engine they are greeted with hugely inflated prices. Many individuals now find themselves with nothing but a pair of running shoes that have seen better days, and the body bestowed to them by Mother Nature.

Meaningless challenges have been tossed around the internet; '6 PAC ABS AT HOME' programmes have been sold which are as vapid as their authors, and forearms have experienced increased hypotrophy in direct correlation to the increasing profits of OnlyFans.

This training programme started with an incredibly simple idea, I wonder if I can do a pull-up from that tree? Through my own experience of over a decade in numerous gyms and knowledge gained from hundreds of hours spent in the great outdoors, I've come to the conclusion that one of the best possible environments to maximise muscle, develop strength, and optimise nutrition is just beyond your front door.

This book will attempt to outline a method of training that uses the environment of the woodland to help you build as much strength and muscle as possible. All you will need is your own body and a selection of logs.

"The mountains, the forest, and the sea, render men savage; they develop the fierce, but yet do not destroy the human" Victor Hugo

With greater knowledge of your training environment comes a greater ability to unlock its secrets. The woodlands of the British Isles have shaped and developed its people since pre-history. The ability to harness its power as a source of great strength has been lost by all but a few.

I believe a brief history of the woodland that has existed in Britain for over a millennia is necessary. If this is of no interest to you, feel free to skip to the next part.

For the last million years, the climate of Britain has been predominantly arctic, with short stages of warmer conditions similar to what we are currently enjoying. The time that has elapsed in Britain since the last glacier period is extremely brief when considered in the wider scheme of things. This intermittent time has allowed for the development of woodland.

At the peak of the last glacial period (approximately 12,000 BC) the majority of Britain and Ireland would have been completely barren of trees.

As the ice started to retreat ever northwards across the island, the emergence of different tree species from the south would have begun. The first most likely specimens were birch, aspen, and sallow, with pine and hazel trees spreading northwards from 8500 BC. The earliest trees were better suited to artic conditions and further specimens would not emerge (such as lime, elm, ash etc.) until warmer climates prevailed.

Before man appeared on the scene, there is much speculation of what form the wilderness of Britain would have taken. The most recent theory speculates that wilderness in the western area of Europe would have been a tapestry of scrub, individual trees, and groups (or groves) of trees. A considerably different environment from what any potential Woodland Warrior will encounter today.

It wouldn't have appeared as closed and impenetrable woodland, instead resembling something more akin to a wildlife park. During earlier times of glacial activity in Britain, legendary Palaeolithic beasts such as bison and wild boar needed large areas of grasslands to fuel their mighty mass. By the time the first human inhabitants of Britain arrived, these types of woodland and the wildlife that inhabited them would have been well established.

The evidence that oak persisted throughout this period is an indication that such animals did indeed graze mainland Britain. Oak requires open ground in order to regenerate; this would have required the natural maintenance provided by grazing. Aurochs, a now extinct form of wild cattle, present in Britain until the bronze-age, were specialists when it came to eating grass, requiring grasslands rather than closed forests.

These early woodlands would have been undisturbed habitats for herbivores for some time, and wouldn't have begun to take on a new purpose until the arrival of the first human beings.

The woodland and the first arrival of humans

The first humans arriving to the British Isles most likely already had knowledge of how to use the natural landscape and woodland that surrounded them in order to survive.

They would have gradually developed expertise in foraging wild edible plants and fungi from woodland and the surrounding habitat. This skill is something that has been tragically forgotten by many who are now dependent on the continuous conveyer belt of mass-produced supermarket fodder.

In 1991, a 5000 year old corpse was found in a glacier in the Alps of Italy. The oldest natural human mummy ever found in Europe, this iceman became famous for the glimpse he gave us into the lives of Copper Age Europeans. We know that he carried two types of mushrooms; the birch polypore (*Piptoporus betulinus*) and another mushroom, most likely to help start a fire, known as the tinder polypore (*Fomes fomentarius*). We can only mostly speculate why Otzi the Iceman would have been carrying these two fungi. Birch polypore has strong medicinal qualities which our ancestors would have been aware of through years of trial and error. This also applies to the tinder polypore, which is also considered to have anti-inflammatory and antibacterial properties.

It's not just wild edibles that would have been utilised; the resources provided from the hunting of the mammals that inhabited the forests, such as red deer, would have been used as much as possible in helping these tribes to prosper. Not only would the meat have been an important source of nutrition, but all parts of the animal would have been used to make items such as tools and clothing.

At the end of the Mesolithic period, different agricultural practices appear to have occurred. There is evidence of an increase in edible wild plants such as stinging nettles and plantain, which indicates more agricultural use of the land as both these floral species thrive alongside human activity.

In some areas, such as the Somerset levels, the population increased dramatically, with virtually all wildwood being cleared as early as 500BC within this area. This existence of truly wildwood would have decreased ever more so as new civilisations and cultures began to emerge in Britain.

Woodland and the civilisations of Britain

Many of the lives of the early inhabitants of Britain would have revolved around the woodland. Not only did their daily routines centre on the passage of the seasons and their products, their imaginations would have been filled with notions surrounding sacred groves and ancestral spirits. Pre-Christian pagan veneration of trees was extensive. Trees and woods are deeply rooted in the psyche of all Europeans. All rural communities would have spun around the axle of wood and woodsmanship during these early times. The Celts had developed the ability to manipulate wood into a fine art, as demonstrated by the remains of houses, boats, and other such artefacts. One can imagine the sounds of an axe, billhook, and a snuffling pig filling the air of most woodland well into the late Middle Ages.

The distribution and management of woodland wouldn't have differed greatly between the Roman occupation of Britain and the arrival of Anglo-Saxons. In more wooded areas, the Anglo-Saxons took over Roman clearings and named them lays. Later they may have created clearings of their own, but the distribution of woodland would not have been dramatically altered. In areas where less woodland persisted, they may have been left undisturbed. Open field strips would have been established and increased agriculture would have created small villages and hamlets.

The woods that remained would have been managed by a process known as 'coppicing'. This is the practice of cutting a particular woodland area every five to thirty years, and therefore ensuring a fresh supply of timber. The practice of coppicing was incredibly important for the next several millennia for building materials, roads, fences, fuel, and metal working. Archaeological evidence demonstrates coppice products were required for numerous rural purposes throughout the Bronze, Roman, and Saxon periods. Coppicing remained the most widespread method of woodland management until the 17th century.

Woodland and worship

We can appreciate the great value placed on woodland areas by the natives of ancient Britain. The woodland played a central role in both practical and spiritual life. The nature of the forest would have evolved and changed with the seasons and reinforced the central role of nature as the master of the universe of which the natives inhabited. The woodland would have often served as the epicentre of the life force from which these communities garnered their strength.

Take the oak tree for example. It is speculated that druids would have viewed this tree as being endowed with the spirits of the gods. The oak tree would thus have been found in abundance amongst sacred groves, where ceremonies of a religious nature, communal gatherings, and legal discussions would have been held. This is a common theme amongst all pagan practices, as trees normally are a central display in such rituals.

The term druid translates to 'tree knowledge'. Many different gods would have been worshipped within their sacred groves, such as the Celtic God Taranis who, much like other European gods of thunder, are associated with the oak tree.

Roman historians and authors of the first and second centuries AD consistently highlighted the connection druids had with what they regarded as 'sacred groves' in the forest, as stated by the roman poet Lucan:

Oh Druids, now that the war is over

You return to your barbaric rites and sinister ways.

You alone know the ways of the gods and the powers of heaven,

Or perhaps you don't know at all.

You who dwell in dark and remote forest groves.

Lucan, Pharsalia, 1.444-46, 450-58

He also provides a description of a forest grove encountered by Cesar:

There stood a grove, which from the earliest time no hand of man had dared to violate;

Hidden from the sun, its chill recesses; matted boughs entwined with prisoned air within.

Stagnant the air, unmoving, yet the leaves filled with mysterious trembling.

Lucan, Pharsalia, 3.399 – 508

These accounts most likely do hold some grain of truth to what religious practices would have been like for the druids at this time. This account would have been tainted with the agenda of the Roman Empire. The Romans sought to paint the native sacred practices of the lands they wished to conquer as being barbaric in nature, with roman occupation being the only solution to create some kind of civilised society amongst these uncivilised people. In reality, the druids were most likely the priestly caste of much of ancient Britain and Gaul. There is strong evidence to suggest that ritualistic sacrifice of some kind did take place, but the admiration and idolisation of forest groves and their importance was likely to be sophisticated.

When Seahenge, a small early Bronze Age timber circle was first discovered, it was made entirely from oak trees. Archaeologists speculate this choice of oak would have been deliberate. Other trees, such as ash or willow, would have served this purpose just as well. Even then, oak was considered the best timber for use in construction, and therefore must have been held in a high regard. Pliny the Elder stated that druids believed that everything that could be found of use on the oak tree was directly sent by God.

It is important to keep in mind that the distinction between everyday life and religious practice would have been far less distinct than it is in the 21st Century. Interaction with nature would have been more central to everyday life, from hunting and harvests to religious Pagan ceremonies and worship. It would have been revered to a degree that we cannot begin to comprehend.

Some remaining Anglo-Saxon texts reveal small details of the spiritual role of trees within this society, and in particular the influence they had over language. The Anglo-Saxon God Woden was said to have hung on the 'Cosmic Tree' in order to find the answer to the riddle of death. In doing so, he in fact discovered the power of the runes. For Anglo-Saxons, there were two runic alphabets comprising of twenty-eight letters. Three of these had the names of trees; ash, yew, and oak.

In terms of worship within sacred groves, it is believed that only one god would have been venerated in a grove at one time, which is in contrast to the ancient Celts. This is reflected in the place name of Thundersley in Essex, which is believed to be the location of worship for the God Thunor, the god of skies and the son of Woden.

The yew and linden tree were also both held in high importance within Anglo-Saxon paganism, with various tribes meeting under such trees for festivals and to seek council. The yew is believed to offer a portal between the world of the living and the world of the dead, hence why yew trees are often found in cemeteries to this day.

Modern day woodland

In 1086 only about 15% of England was woodland or wood-pasture; 35% was arable, 30% pasture, 1% hay meadow and the remaining 20% was mountain, moor, heath, fen or urban land.

The Domesday Book of 1086 is evidence that every wood in England belonged to some person or some community. Many woods were 'exclaves' owned by communities some miles away. The fact that it was worth transporting the woodland produce over some distance indicates their value, and that ownership had been established long previously.

The Domesday landscape was more like modern day Britain than the untamed woodland of folklore. Nearly all woods were highly managed, as coppices or wood pastures.

Over the next several hundred years, woodland in Britain would continue to decrease. Woodland cover in England was below 5% by 1870. What remained of ancient woodland was destroyed through continued agricultural use and conifer plantations, particularly after 1945. Estimates suggest that nearly half of the remaining ancient woodlands of Britain were seriously damaged or obliterated by 1975. In that 30-year period alone there was more damage to woodland than in the past 1000 years.

By the beginning of the 20th century about 90% of all timber was imported. The bulk of this arrived from America and Scandinavia.

The forestry commission in 1919 aimed to ensure that a shortage of timber wasn't experienced again (the First World War had sent demand soaring). By 1939 the commission had established 230 forests on about 265,000 hectares of land. These were predominantly timber of a fast-growing nature, such as conifers. These young plantations were too immature to provide materials for the Second World War in 1945, and consequently 524,000 acres of private land was felled to meet the demand.

During the last decade in the 20th century, there has been great change in forestry commission policy. The U.K. commitment to biodiversity following the Rio Earth Summit (1992) has resulted in biodiversity actions plans being drawn up by the government. Grants are now given towards encouraging the natural regeneration of Britain's ancient woodland. Coppicing is making a return as a renewable method of woodland management. The Woodland Trust now co-ordinates grants towards tree and hedgerow planting, as well as the creation of ponds and further habitats. Hopefully these developments mean a brighter and bigger future for the woodlands of Britain.

"There is a serene and settled majesty to woodland scenery that enters into the soul and delights and elevates it, and fills it with noble inclinations." Washington Irving

I've always noticed a near direct correlation between my own well-being and the amount of time I spend in woodland. I believe one of the biggest mistakes in our modern day thought processes is that we are somehow separate and above nature. This is a complete fallacy; we are nature. We are the product of its primordial soup. We are not outside of it, but a part of it, no matter how much we try to fool ourselves with our sharp suits and elaborate technology that this is not the case. To return and embed ourselves within its embrace as frequently as we can will help us to manifest our greater selves.

As I'm not one for simply mumbling esoteric outbursts, and am an empiricist at heart, in this chapter I'll outline some of the reasons why being in nature can help all our gainz.

The modern world and the dislocation from nature

It often feels like everything we are surrounded by, from the moment we wake up to the point when we seek the solitude of our beds, is designed to distract. From the smartphone to the latest games console, we have become addicted to activities that provide a rush of dopamine, all of which often occur behind closed doors.

Compared to our ancient tribal ancestors, I imagine most people now only spend a minuscule fraction of their time outside. At no point will I suggest that it is always possible to un-plug from a world that is now constantly plugged in whether we like it or not. That being said, I truly believe that there is a better balance to be found. On average, all of us spend 2.25 hours on our smart phones every day. That's approximately 34 days in a year. In an average lifetime, that equates to roughly 7 years of your life spent looking at a pixelated screen, and that isn't even including a television or a computer. At some point all our tombstones will simply read: 'Here lays iPhone 24 user 001101'.

We no longer experience natural environments enough to realise how restored our very being can feel from just a small regular increase in our time spent outside. We are also oblivious to the numerous studies that are clearly proving that nature makes us stronger, more creative, more empathetic, and more able to engage constructively with the world as a whole.

But we don't need modern science to point this out to us. Ancient Greek philosophers such as Aristotle proclaimed that his frequent walks outside allowed him to clear his mind. The pioneer of evolutionary theory Charles Darwin was renowned for taking frequent walks in his garden and groves to help him think. The great philosopher Immanuel Kant was so well known for taking a walk at the same time each day that local residents would often set their watches based upon this behaviour. So you get the idea, go for a walk.

Aristotle would teach while walking in the open air of the Lyceum. Nietzsche proclaimed that "all truly great thoughts are conceived while walking". Anticipating the nature and exercise debate before it even truly occurred, Thoreau stated in his essay 'Walking': "I think that I cannot preserve my health and spirits, unless I spend four hours a day at least- and it is commonly more than that- sauntering through the woods and over the hills and fields, absolutely free from all worldly engagements".

Teddy Roosevelt would take what was known as 'nature baths', simply strolling around in the nude outside. The whole Romantic Movement was built upon the idea that nature was the key to humanity's salvation. The poet Wordsworth wrote of a fusing of 'the round ocean and the living air, and the blue sky and in the mind of Man'. Beethoven would hug a linden tree in his back garden for motivation. This may all sound a bit flocculent, but they were practising what science has now proven, that our nervous systems are designed to correspond to stimulus that we find within nature.

The biophilia effect

I think all of us know deep down that nature is intrinsically good for us. Almost like an intuition that it is where we truly belong. In Japan they have a word for a feeling like this: *Yugen.* It communicates a profound sense of the overwhelming beauty and mystery of the universe.

In Japan, there is a practice known as forest-bathing, or '*shinrin yoku*' in Japanese. It's a simple practice of retreating to the forest to be within nature. The focus is on connecting with the forest physically by engaging one's senses of sight, hearing, taste, touch, and smell. The idea with forest bathing is to let nature entirely into your body, based upon ancient Shinto and Buddhist practices.

The biophilia hypothesis suggests that after our evolutionary ancestors survived being chased by some kind of predator, the peaceful and more nurturing elements of nature would have had a soothing effect. Immersing ourselves within nature helps to subside the adrenaline coursing through our veins and return our bodies to a calm homeostasis.

The biophilia theory relies on the correct notion that we have spent 99.9% of our evolutionary time in nature, the conclusion being that it must play a rather large part in our overall well-being.

Anthropologist Yoshifumi Miyazaki has undertaken extensive research into the benefits of woodland walks. Using thousands of his research students as participants, he compared stress levels, as indicated by their hormone levels, during a walk in an urban environment and a walk within a forest. He discovered that the woodland stroll delivered a 12% reduction in cortisol levels whereas the urban walk increased cortisol levels by 22%.

Japanese researcher Dr Qing Li conducted a study with 8 businessmen from Tokyo. They hiked for three days in forest environment. By the end of the experiment the blood tests revealed that their white blood cell count had increased by up to 40%, with this boast lasting for the following 7 days.

Soil and Fungi

It may not be just the sensory information gained from the woodland that plays a role in increasing overall well-being. Studies have attributed health benefits to soil compounds like actinomycetes. In two separate experiments in the U.K. in 2010, mice exposed to fungal compounds within soil showed an increased ability to solve a maze, demonstrated less anxiety and had increased levels of the neurotransmitter serotonin. Luckily enough for us, exposure to both soil and fungi is guaranteed in the Woodland Warrior method.

Studies on human well-being and nature are still very much in their infancy. Thirty years ago, the science on how physical activity affects overall physical health and neurological well-being was only in its beginning stages, with many individuals sceptical about the true extent of how exercise could be of such a huge benefit. As we thankfully now know, they couldn't have been more wrong.

Bring back your attention

It could be possible that these positive effects of being in nature are emerging to a greater degree as the modern world increases its hold over our attention. Perhaps a woodland environment offers a form of mindfulness. When you're engaged in nature, and leave your smart phone behind, the mind becomes more passive and peaceful. The world, for the first time in an age, begins to come and go as it should in your sensory perception.

When we aren't looking at our phone a hundred and fifty times a day, we begin to wake up for the first time from our technology induced slumber. At no point am I trying to over romanticise the lives of our Neolithic ancestors, imagining them skipping through ancient woodlands building up their deltoids and engaging in brotherly rituals. Mortality rates were likely higher, and they had the ever present phantom of not knowing where their next meal would come from. One stops to question if this existence did have more value in some aspects. Despite the benefits that our modern times do have in comparison, the value of being in nature is becoming increasingly clearer.

Be more like a Finn

In Finland, there still exists to this day a culture enriched with outdoor experiences. For the Finnish, an expression of their identity as a community is closely linked with nature. They are a nation obsessed with mushroom hunting, berry picking, fishing, lake swimming and Nordic skiing.

According to large surveys carried out within Finland, the average Finn engages in nature based recreation at least two to three times per week. 58% of Finns go berry picking, 35% cross country ski, and 70% regularly hike. In comparison, only 30% of most Americans and Europeans spend their time hiking.

It appears we have a considerable amount to learn from the Finns. It could be easy to state that the Finns are in an arrested state of development, in terms of their apparent resistance to wide sweeping technological modernisation. But I believe this purely shows how other cultures have become overdeveloped, with what could be claimed is a now crippling dependence on technology.

Finland is helped by the fact that it was incredibly late in experiencing large scale urbanisation. It wasn't until the sixties and seventies that a large number of Finns decided to relocate to the city. Before this mass migration, they were considered 'forest people'. Many Finns still have a grandparent who lives on a farm or woodlot. It's no surprise that Finland scores highly on global scales of happiness when you consider the amount of time they spend outdoors.

Finland is the most forested country in Europe with 74% of its entire mass covered in trees. The forests are mostly privately owned, but the concept of trespassing doesn't really exist. Finnish law operates under the idea of '*jokamiehenoikeus*', or 'everyman's right'. This means that anyone can walk, forage and camp on anyone else's property. The only things you can't do are cut timber and kill game. Regardless of your opinion on the concept of private property, the freedom to access woodland like this anywhere else in the world is extremely rare. Whether the concept of '*jokamiehenoikeus*' would work in all cultures and nations is entirely up for debate.

In one study conducted in Finland, 3000 city dwellers were questioned on their emotional and restorative experiences in nature. They discovered that the biggest boosts occurred after five hours a month in natural settings. The more time people spent in green areas, the better they reported feeling. This was highest amongst groups who spent time in the forest. Participants who spent much of this time in the woodland felt 20% better than their urban peers.

The role of sunlight and Vitamin D

You will be filled with a new sense of energy when the sun hits your back as you perform your pull-ups from the nearest oak tree.

And this effect is no placebo. Approximately 90% of the body's vitamin D comes from the action of sunlight on the skin, which results in the synthesis of vitamin D in the body. It doesn't take much to discover that the reduction of this synthesis can be correlated with a reluctance to venture outdoors.

Low production of vitamin D in the body during the winter months can contribute towards feelings of low mood and despair which often accompany dark winter evenings. It is no coincidence that countries in the northern hemisphere (Iceland being one example) which experience particular short daylight hours see Vitamin D supplementation as a crucial habit.

Numerous studies have highlighted the benefits of maximising the presence of vitamin D in the human body. Vitamin D helps maintain bone mineralisation by ensuring levels of calcium remain high within the bloodstream. This is achieved by increasing the absorption of dietary calcium from the large and small intestines. Vitamin D also greatly helps prevent colds and strains of the flu, possibly something of great importance considering current events.

This increased solar absorption will also boost your testosterone. One study discovered a correlation between vitamin D deficiency and low testosterone. When participants spent more time in the sun, their testosterone levels increased in correlation with the levels of vitamin D in their bloodstream. Start seeing the sun as your best anabolic companion.

The mind and the body

The estimate for the number of deaths worldwide annually due to a lack of physical activity is 1.9 million. In preindustrial times, we expended on average one thousand calories per day due to greater physical demands; now it's barely more than three hundred calories. We can all perform exercise outdoors, but as demonstrated, a woodland environment provides you with so much more. When you combine exercise and nature, the positive effects are much greater in magnitude. A return to the sacred groves is long overdue.

The woodland environment provides a sanctuary for not only the mind, but the body. I imagine I don't necessarily need to now reel off all the benefits of physical activity. And this activity doesn't simply have to be some form of resistance training or advanced calisthenics. A longer life span can be achieved even by simply walking. Studies have demonstrated that even just walking for forty minutes a day could protect the aging brain from cognitive decline. If you combine this with the restorative sanctuary of the forest, you've got a winning formula.

Over the last several decades, a large proportion of society has been conditioned to believe that exercising must be conducted within a gym. Without the ritual commute, changing rooms, towel, and treadmills, you haven't really done any exercise. Heaven forbid if this isn't also accompanied by a sweaty selfie and gym shark leggings. The woodland can be one of the most valuable tools to mould our bodies into the lean and dynamic mechanism of nature that it was truly meant to be.

"For me life is continuously being hungry. The meaning of life is not simply to exist, to survive, but to move ahead, to go up, to achieve, to conquer" Arnold Schwarzenegger

Developing an increased amount of muscle tissue in the body is both incredibly simple on one hand, and quite complex on the other. If your body is exposed to progressive forms of stress in the form of some kind of resistance movement, then provided with adequate recovery, you're more than likely to add muscle mass. That being said, numerous variables will greatly impact this ability to add muscle.

One aspect that many modern fitness professionals fail to explain adequately or choose to ignore all together is that the amount of muscle mass you can carry (excluding performance enhancing compounds) is largely genetically pre-determined.

If you choose to look at photos of Arnold Schwarzenegger, Jay Cutler, Ronnie Coleman, Dorian Yates or Lee Priest at the ages of fifteen, before some form of anabolic steroid use, they will still put most enhanced gym rats to absolute shame.

Genes can affect things as integral to building muscle as your skeletal structure, muscle belly attachments, types of muscle fibres, and myostatin levels.

I've frequently been accused of steroid use. As I approach my 30th Birthday, I've been training naturally since the age of sixteen. I can also count on one hand the amount of training sessions in the gym I've missed in over a decade. This 'enhanced' natural look may purely be down to genes and being exposed to some form of awkward heavy load carrying from an early age.

There is some evidence from research in epigenetics that suggests the behaviour and choices of our ancestors has an impact on the structure of our genetic code. It could be possible that the long lineage of my family working in agriculture has affected me thus.

The physiques of Eugen Sandow or John Grimek predates the synthesis and distribution of anabolic steroids. These two individuals are testaments to the potential of the natural physique. Genetics not only apply to the amount of muscle mass you are attempting to gain, but also strength. A bigger muscle is a stronger muscle, or at least has a larger area from which to access surface tension or to decrease the distance the bar must travel in lifts such as the bench press. Leverages are of great importance in powerlifting. Someone with a short torso but long arms will most likely be gifted for the deadlift. Someone with short arms and a thick torso will be gifted for the bench press. Distribution of both type 1 and type 2 muscle fibres may also dictate how strong you can become.

Don't become defeatist at this revelation. Regardless of an individual's genetics, we all have the ability to add more muscle mass to our frames. Genes may end up simply meaning an inch difference in the circumference of your arms or five to ten extra kilograms on the barbell. Granted, this may mean the difference between defeat and glory at your local powerlifting meet, but such is life. It's a cliché, but simply focus on gaining the best physique you possibly can and the greatest level of strength you can obtain naturally. Don't cry yourself to sleep at night or feel sorry for yourself simply because eighteen-inch arms or a three plate bench may be forever outside of your grasp.

I have zero moral objections to the use of performance enhancing drugs, provided you don't claim to be natural. The disadvantage your genetics have given you can be circumvented to an extent by PED's of various kinds, but not completely. I've still witnessed natural athletes out bench the largest enhanced lifters.

How muscles grow

I strongly believe the Woodland Warrior method will be successful in adding lean muscle and strength, but you will have to be the ultimate judge of that. Feel free to skip this section where I explain the basic science of muscle building. It may not teach you anything you don't already know.

Muscles grow by repairing tiny tears, these tears occur on a cellular level when exposed to some kind of stimulus from resistance training. This resistance could be of any kind, simply a strenuous form of bodyweight training or heavy loads provided by typical gym equipment. These tears tell the body to send extra blood flow to the affected area, bringing with it the ingredients needed for repair that will make it larger and stronger than it was previously. This is known as muscle protein synthesis. The rate of muscle protein synthesis has to be less than that of muscle protein breakdown in your body in order for growth to occur.

Strength training doesn't create new muscle cells; it increases the size of these cells. It's thanks to this increase in size that you will begin to witness a more aesthetically pleasing physique. All progression in the size of your muscles will most likely correlate with progression in your strength. This is achieved through a combination of metabolic stress, muscle damage, and mechanical tension.

Mechanical tension and muscle damage

Mechanical tension is simply the term used to describe when your muscles are being put under tension by some kind of load, whether from a barbell or bodyweight training. Metabolic stress is the process of oxygen depletion within the muscle during training so when you reach failure, you will recruit more fast twitch muscle fibres. Without these two basic components, increasing muscle mass will prove to be nearly impossible.

Muscle damage (a result of mechanical tension and metabolic stress) can appear as the feeling of soreness you experience anywhere from 24 to 72 hours after your workout, otherwise known as delayed onset muscle soreness, or DOM's for short. This is most likely to happen when you introduce a new stimulus into your training or you haven't trained for some time. The verdict on whether muscle soreness is a clear sign of growth is still some-what disputed within the sports science community. The common sense prediction may well be that if you've damaged the muscle cells enough to induce inflammation and soreness, the body will engage some kind of repair in response. The negative aspect to this may be that if the body isn't adequately rested or provided with nutrition to help in this process, and soreness persists frequently after every strength training session regardless of the stimulus, then it may be indicator that you're recovery protocol needs re-evaluating.

Successful training for the Woodland Warrior

While we've seen the basic pre-requisites for muscle building, it is also important that we are aware of how this looks in practicality. I will outline what I believe to be some of the key tenants of how to build a glorious physique based upon my own opinion and what I believe to be the key mantras of some of the greats of physical culture:

1. Consistency
2. Intensity
3. Progress
4. Autoregulation

Consistency

Following a structured training programme, whether it requires you to complete a workout three, four, or five times a week, is of the up-most importance. The muscles need to be regularly exposed to this trauma in order to grow. Completing a workout every other Monday isn't going to cut it. Ensuring you've completed what is required to match your goals in the specific time frame given is essential. If you're a natural lifter this is of particular importance. I also believe that any one muscle group in the body needs to be trained at least twice in a seven to ten day period. So for example, upper body dedicated sessions twice a week, followed by two lower body sessions twice a week, which is exactly what this training programme will advocate.

If you miss two workouts every four weeks, and you're scheduled to train four times a week, that's twenty-four workouts in a year. So roughly six weeks of training time in total. I can guarantee that this will affect your progress regardless of your goals. These workouts could mean the difference between success and failure.

Intensity

Intensity can be something that's quite hard to measure. I'm not necessarily referring to techniques such as supersets or negatives and shorter rest periods, which are good methods to increase the difficulty of a workout. Intensity can be difficult to judge due to its subjectivity. One person may find one of the workouts within the beginners programme in this book incredibly challenging and will be able to say with some confidence that they are giving maximum effort.

Another may simply find it too easy and know for a fact they need to move on to the intermediate or advanced programme. You will have little chance of building muscle if you don't find your training challenging, regardless of any techniques you apply. There isn't any secret formula to working hard, just be honest with yourself and use the experience gained from following a structured programme to begin to listen to your body. You will need to find the right balance between training hard enough to create enough stimuli for muscle growth but not to get injured or suffer burn out. You want to get close to failure on the majority of the exercises that will be prescribed. Failure in this context means you are unable to perform repetition with correct form. The programme will specify when this is required.

Any set that is taken to failure will have to recruit slow twitch muscle fibres, after which they will begin to recruit fast twitch muscle fibres. When the force required by your muscles to move your own body or that particular object can no longer be met you will have reached failure. The closer you get to failure in the movement, the faster twitch muscle fibres are recruited to a greater extent. These fibres have the ability to achieve approximately 50% more growth than slow twitch fibres.

Progress

Progress within this programme will be measured by a combination of both objective and subjective methods. Objective methods being things such as your weight increasing or decreasing (depending upon your goals) and the amount you can lift and/or the number of repetitions you can perform of any given movement. It will be important to keep a record of these numbers over time.

Subjective methods include what you see in the mirror and comments from others. I'm not trying to promote some form of vanity, but having a strong and lean physique normally comes with aesthetic appeal.

When it comes to progress, there are some basic questions that greet us. Take number of repetitions for example. We have all probably experienced by this stage that 8-12 repetitions is often advocated as the ideal repetition range for muscle hypertrophy. But in reality a combination of both higher and lower repetitions is our best course of action. This programme will use a wide range of repetitions. Progressive overload will be our main focus to ensure a long term investment in muscular gains.

Due to the fact we will be utilising the timber that surrounds us in the forest, there will be some subjectivity to the exact weight of this load that we wouldn't find with barbells and plates. That being said, we will be experiencing different densities and sizes of timber that will allow us to vary the load we are using. Through gradual experience we will be able to select logs that provide the appropriate challenge for that exercise and repetition requirements.

Research suggests that as long as muscular failure is achieved, repetitions as high as forty will promote muscle growth. Higher repetitions can be useful for when we reach a plateau. This will be useful for bodyweight movements as a variable that can be adapted due to the fact that we can't increase the load the muscle is under, unless our bodyweight increases or we use some kind of added weight, such as a weighted vest.

Auto-regulation

This may be something that those among us with less training might struggle to comprehend, but I believe it's one of the most important aspects to success in the long term.

Autoregulation is your ability to adapt your training to how your body is feeling on that specific day or time period. The illusion that the fitness industry often perpetuates is that you should follow your training programme without any flexibility whatsoever. I do recommend that your training protocol is followed as much as possible, but if there is a choice between not training and doing some form of activity, then the latter is the better choice. Take the upper body workout I did today for example. I had log over-head press but for whatever reason my left shoulder was experiencing pain, to the point where I couldn't perform the movement correctly. Instead of persevering, which some would have recommended in this instance, I simply performed a less intense isolation exercise of dumbbell lateral raises. Not my first choice, because as you will soon discover, I believe compound movements like the overhead press provide adequate stimulus for entire shoulder development.

The main danger when applying autoregulation is a lack of self-discipline. This isn't simply a concept that you can apply when you're simply not feeling it or you're suffering from a hangover. It takes a detailed understanding of your own body and knowing when to adapt appropriately to either avoid injury, or to ensure you can complete your next scheduled workout. It won't suit those inclined to laziness or those afraid of some discomfort. Be strict with yourself and regulate your own training for circumstances such as the above. This will come with experience, so a beginner is unlikely to be able to apply this concept immediately. Regardless of your current fitness levels, you can't give your maximum effort all of the time.

The motivation myth

If you're in any way a fan of physical culture, from bodybuilding to strongman, you will no doubt be bombarded with memes, quotes, and videos that include the word motivation within the title. You will either be greeted by some utter nonsense such as 'you have to believe to achieve' or a reel of enhanced bodybuilders.

It's a mistake to place your likelihood of success or failure purely on how 'motivated' you feel on that specific day. I do not doubt that motivation exists, but it's a fleeting emotion. Like fear or anger. Of course I feel a stronger desire to train when I see a montage of a powerlifter I admire hitting several personal records in a row. These feelings can and probably should play a small role in the cocktail of ingredients of why you choose to exercise. Your long-term success can't rely on something as impermanent as motivation. You need to discover an intrinsic value to why you're doing what you're doing. In this context, engaging in a training programme to develop your physique should be connected with long term goals of your choice. One assumes these could be things as simple as health and longevity or a greater ability to perform both general and specialist tasks of a physically demanding nature.

I guarantee days will come where you lack energy and want to seek comfort in things that provide short term satisfaction such as a Netflix binge and all the fast food you can afford. Motivation will be nowhere in sight. It's on these days that you need to focus on the long term picture and on goals that are intrinsic in value; that's what will get you back into the woods.

Further practical considerations for the Woodland Warrior

Training volume within the Woodland Warrior programme will naturally increase between the three different programmes. This is an important aspect to your progression when it comes to adding new muscle and strength. If you want to maximise muscle growth, then total volume should increase over time. A careful combination of quality and quantity is required.

This won't appear quite as simple as just increasing the number of repetitions and sets. Warm up sets aside, each working set should be challenging. You will often hear 'mind muscle connection' thrown around in bodybuilding circles with a certain amount of mysticism surrounding it. It's made far more obscure than it needs to be, all it actually involves is focusing your mind on the specific muscle you are trying to target during that particular movement. You will find as you advance through the programmes, more muscle groups will be targeted within a week when compared to the beginners programme. This is why tracking your progress will inform the next steps you take. A muscle will have to adapt to a new stimulus in order to continue to grow.

Traditional bodybuilding approaches often rely upon splitting up different body parts, such as Monday being chest and triceps, and Wednesday being shoulders and biceps. It is my opinion that for the majority, this isn't the most optimal approach. If you're looking to get as aesthetic and strong as possible, then focusing on major muscle groups and compounds movements is your best course of action. The minimum amount one movement pattern that's designed to cause some kind of growth should be performed at least twice a week. Exercise induced muscle growth doesn't last more than three to four days on average. This is one of the main reasons why a 'bro' split may not be the most effective method.

Overtraining is also another term you will hear quite often, but I find it a bit misleading. I would choose to think of it as 'under-recovery'. Your training needs to match your ability to recover. Overtraining would require huge amounts of stress, that some would argue is only really possible for professional athletes. In my experience, the majority of individuals appear to not fully comprehend the work required to obtain a lean and muscular physique in the first place, or know what it is to require some kind of advanced training method.

If this advanced stage is reached, they then often overestimate what it takes to maintain these results. At some point, and this mostly only applies to those who are training naturally without the assistance of any performance enhancing drugs, we will all reach our full potential when it comes to the amount of muscle we can carry, and the loads we can lift.

From this point, establishing what form of training and nutrition will help us maintain the maximum amount of development will take some form of experimentation and experience. But it will almost certainly look quite different to what got you there in the first place. This is purely conjecture on my part, and I don't believe this apex of development occurs until you've at least achieved a decade of dedicated training.

When it comes to rest periods, the most common mind-set is resting short periods for muscle growth and longer periods for maximum attempts, like the kind of thing you will see in powerlifting.

Short rest periods in bodybuilding are often associated with higher metabolic stress, and would therefore cause a greater growth stimulus for the muscle.

Regardless of goals, research is demonstrating that longer rest periods are superior when compared to shorter rest periods. One study compared the rest period of three minutes versus one minute. The group who rested for three minutes had a clear advantage over the group that rested for one minute. They also developed greater muscle tissue thickness in the long term. This will apply to all exercises suggested within the Woodland Warrior programme. There will be specific considerations we need to make due to the nature of the programme. As it is an outdoor based training system, some type of activity may be required during your rest periods if low temperatures are a factor. This can be as simple as walking. The type of exercise you are performing from the programme will also play a role. For example, pull-ups, (which are a multi-joint exercise that asks a lot of the neuromuscular system) will require at least two minutes rest (or less if you feel up to it). Compare this with most core exercises which are less metabolically stressful that can be performed with just one minutes rest. Don't be tempted to start scrolling through Instagram during these rest periods; use them wisely to observe the woodland before you.

"The charm of a woodland road lies not only in its beauty but in anticipation. Around each bend may be a discovery, an adventure" Dale Rex Coman

The woodland will no longer be purely the place you take your partner for a Sunday stroll after lunch, or where you take your dog for its compulsory thirty minutes of exercise per day. It will now become your sanctuary of strength.

Gyms are sometimes referred to as the Temple of Iron; in that case welcome to the Temple of Timber. All you're going to need is access to some kind of public woodland. It might be handy to bring an axe along, but it isn't essential. This also applies to rope, if certain branches prove unreachable and you want to try rope pull-ups or you need to create handles for your logs.

The entire Woodland Warrior training system will be split into what I consider to be a beginner, intermediate, and advanced programme. They will be presented in order, and in keeping with the name sake of the entire method, will hereby be known as the Hawthorn, Hazel, and Oak programmes. A hawthorn tree is but a shrub; a hazel has strong sturdy limbs but dominates only the hedgerow, whereas an oak is renowned for its strength and position as a lord of the forest.

Physical culture

Physical culture has a tradition that dates back thousands of years, before 24 hour gyms, online coaches or Instagram.

I think we can probably say with some speculation that at some point prehistoric man thought it would be a good test of strength to hang from a branch and try pull-ups. Woodland probably did serve as physical training grounds in some cases. Whether for sheer practical purposes, such as the effort required to chop wood, or to train in some way for competition or combat.

From 10,000 BC, man would have followed a path of physical development that was predetermined by natural law. The need to avoid threats and meet the practical demands of life would have had demanded an almost constant state of locomotion, with the manipulation of awkward natural objects and the development of tools. Pre-historic man would have had to run, climb, jump, balance, crawl, lift, carry, throw, and fight. To state the relatively obvious, the strength and agility of early man would not have relied upon a structured programme of physical training. It is likely with the advent of agriculture that physical activity didn't necessarily decrease but nature of the activity did.

Ancient civilisations, such as the Babylonians, Egyptians, Persians and later on the Greeks and Romans, all prescribed some kind of physical training to their youth. This would have been to primarily prepare them for battle. Carrying awkward heavy objects like stones and logs, as well as unarmed combat would have been a common occurrence.

It is in this spirit of these ancient methods of physical training that we will venture forth.

The programmes

This programme will be a mixture of calisthenics, interval based conditioning, weighted resistance using various sizes and forms of logs, as well as some exercises that are based on being able to train either with someone else or in a group. It will include the flexibility to exclude some of these elements, such as the group training. From the Hawthorn programme to the Oak programme, it will encourage basic linear progression over time. This programme will not introduce you to any revolutionary new movements or exercises. Although I think I can safely say I haven't seen a training programme so far that has tree climbs for conditioning.

It may just be something you visit when you are away and have access to woodland for a period of time, even if just for a few days. That being said, if you do have unlimited access to woodland, you can follow the programme to the absolute letter if you wish. Its main purpose is to get you out in the woods and engaging with nature through physical fitness.

The Hawthorn Programme

There are certain prerequisites required before beginning any stage of the Woodland Warrior training programme. It assumes you can at least perform three pull-ups and eight press ups. It will also make the assumption that you are mobile and able to perform all exercises in all movement plains. It will rest upon the premise that you're not currently moderately obese and can at least run at a moderate pace for 15 to 20 minutes.

I'll explain certain aspects of the programme in detail and briefly touch upon what I believe to be the correct technique in basic movements, like a press-up or a pull-up. I strongly suggest you read through the entire programme, from Hawthorne to Oak, before embarking on any of them. There are elements from each programme that you may want to incorporate sooner, which you have the freedom to do. These include exercises such as the isolation movements or some of the group activities and circuits. The Hawthorne programme will be incredibly simple. If you are truly a beginner, or at least unaccustomed to a structured training programme, habit building is our top priority.

All the exercises should and will be familiar to you to some degree. Getting used to training four times a week on a regular basis is essential. The Hawthorne programme will introduce you to some of the key movements for the Woodland Warrior method which will be progressed through both the Hazel and Oak stages. Purely for the purposes of what I believe to be both simplicity and effectiveness, workouts will be labelled upper body and lower body. This doesn't necessarily mean this distinction will be closely adhered to. For example, core may be completed in either upper or lower days, as well as some conditioning.

If you find out or can currently see that the Hawthorn programme will be below your current ability level, either increase the intensity or volume to suit you, or skip straight to the Hazel or Oak programme.

Precautions

It goes without saying; you will need access to woodland. The large majority of woodland is privately owned in England. How this compares to other parts of the globe, I'm unsure. Please have an understanding of laws surrounding access to private property wherever you are based. For example, even within the British Isles laws can vary; in Scotland you have freedom to access any land, in England this isn't the case.

If you do have woodland nearby and you know it isn't in public ownership, then seek the landowner's permission. From my perspective as a landowner, if your request appears genuine, and you explain that it's for the purpose of physical activity, then I assume the majority of requests will be granted. But respect the landowner's decision either way and avoid trespassing at all costs.

Some woodland may well be in public ownership, or under the jurisdiction of a body like the woodland trust, the forestry commission, or the national trust. Particularly in regards to the first two, they are often used for recreational activities without permission needed. When it comes to national trust estates, a membership is normally required. Keep in mind poor old Tarquin and Elizabeth might get a bit of a shock if you are seen pressing a tree overhead topless in the distance while they are trying to have a picnic with Mummy and Daddy. If you take a break in a place like the New Forest in the UK, with its ample camping sites and access to thousands of acres of ancient woodland, you shouldn't have any problem whatsoever.

Do not under any circumstances cut down any trees. In any woodland there should be hundreds of fallen branches and logs to choose from, particularly after a storm. An axe will only be required to chop up larger logs if needed to create the size of the log you will require. The Woodland Warrior wants to preserve the biodiversity of the forest, not decrease it.

Be aware that no programme of physical activity is devoid of all risk. In preparation for The Woodland Warrior, I experimented with collecting various logs. When pressing one log overhead, I dropped it on my face and split my lip open. Thankfully that's the only injury I've sustained but it shows you must take care. When it comes to the tree climbs as part of your conditioning, regardless of your current gymnastic qualifications, don't be an idiot and choose a forty metre high beech tree. Aim for something no more than ten metres at a maximum. That doesn't mean you might not fall from time to time, so apologies in advance for any broken bones.

There will be very specific precautions in regards to picking wild edibles for the nutrition aspect of Woodland Warrior; I will focus on these in part 5.

The LMH Log

As we can't weigh the logs (you can go to the trouble if you want), we will use a system based on repetitions to determine our choice of log for different exercises and sets. LMH simply stands for light, medium, and heavy. AMRAP, which is a term you will see quite often, stands for 'as many reps as possible'. This is the number of reps you can perform correctly until failure. This is something that you will have to record to monitor progress and to judge your log selection going forward. You won't necessarily have to source a new log, for example your medium log may become your light log by the time you reach the Hazel or Oak programme. You won't require the heavy log in the Hawthorn programme. There may be times when you will need two of each type of log, which I will specify in each programme description. This will appear as L/M/H respectively.

Light log	AMRAP 15-20 repetitions	Change at 20+ repetitions
Medium log	AMRAP 8-12 repetitions	Change at 12+ repetitions
Heavy log	AMRAP 1-6 repetitions	Change at 6 + repetitions

Type of log and density

You may have logs that are very similar sizes but due to the difference in density between different trees, their weight may vary considerably. The type of wood isn't of great importance, but if you're curious, here is a handy guide to the density of the most common types of trees you are likely to come across in the British Isles, starting with the heaviest first. I will include a description of the bark; I suggest if you want to know what trees are which, you perform further research of your own. There are many books that provide a guide to the trees of Great Britain and Europe. This will also come handy for the section on nutrition. This is not an extensive list, and you may end up using timber that isn't listed below. The main objective is to find a light, medium, and heavy log to get you started.

Species	*Density Kg/m3*	*Description of Bark*
Beech	720	Dark grey smooth bark.
Oak	720	Broad crowned with a stout trunk. Brownish with deep horizontal fissures
Ash	710	Silver grey bark fissured into irregular plates
Birch	670	White with horizontally peeling bark and pinkish markings
Walnut	670	Dark grey with deeply fissured irregular shaped plates
Yew	670	Reddish-brown with purple tones and peeling
Chestnut	560	Dark heavy ridges normally arranged in a spiral pattern
Elm	560	Mature bark is hard, grey-brown and deeply fissured into a pattern of irregular plates
Douglas Fir	530	Deeply fissured and rugged. Younger trees will appear to have blisters that exude resin

One practical consideration to make with your entire log selection is the fact that you will need to get the log onto your upper back or chest. If you're training with a partner, life is made easier and you can get assistance. The best method I've found for getting either my medium or heavy log on to my back is similar to the method used when performing a Steinborn Squat. Rest the end of your log on an elevated surface; it will most likely be some kind of tree trunk in this case. Balance the log with one hand and squat down so the log now rests on either your left or right shoulder. Grab the other end of the log while simultaneously standing up. The log should come with you and now rest on the upper traps, ready to perform either a press or some kind of squat.

The Hawthorn programme is designed to last four weeks. It is predominantly bodyweight based when compared with the Hazel and Oak programmes. It is possible for you to continue on this programme for up to eight weeks. If you feel like you are still making progress come the fourth week then continue.

If at any point you have to take an extended absence from training, then you can return to the Woodland Warrior with the Hawthorn programme if required. The programme is split into two blocks of two weeks, with two upper body sessions and two lower body sessions each week. If you for whatever reason can't commit to four sessions in seven days, simply extend this to ten days. As stated previously, this programme assumes you have some basic knowledge of how to perform certain exercises, such as a burpee. I will indicate where I have gone into more detail on a particular movement. The reps column may also include a time, rather than a number of repetitions; this means you just perform that movement for the allotted time.

Before every workout I do suggest that you do some kind of warmup. I've never been a strong believer of having to limber oneself up for 45 minutes followed by an hour of foam rolling. Some of you may have to walk a distance to your desired woodland and this could suffice as your warmup, especially in the summer. However, during colder months the warmup will be of greater importance. I also advocate overall movement prior to a workout which resembles some of the exercises you will actually perform rather than static or dynamic stretching. Below you will find the warmup routine; I suggest completing this prior to any of the workouts regardless of difficulty level.

Warm up for all Woodland Warrior workouts

Exercise	Sets	Reps	Notes
High Knees	1	20 seconds	Stay on the balls of your feet
Burpees	1	20 seconds	Make sure you explode up into the air on the second part of the movement
Press-ups	1	20 seconds	Make sure arms are fully locked out at the top of the movement
Bodyweight Squats	1	20 seconds	The back of the hamstring must go just below knee level

The Hawthorn Programme

Further explanation of each exercise will be given. Refer to part 7 for photo demonstrations.

Hawthorn upper body 1A weeks 1 & 2

Exercise	Sets	Reps	Notes
Push-ups*	3	8/8*/AMRAP	*5 second holds on the last 3 reps when elbows are at 90 degrees. AMRAP – as many reps as possible until failure. Record.
Tree Pull-ups	3	3/3/AMRAP	Upper chest to the branch, your AMRAP may be below 3, don't worry this is simply due to fatigue.
Close Grip Push-ups	3	8/8/8	Hand placement closer together
Chin-ups	3	3/3/3	Pull-ups and chin-ups are often confused. Please refer to the images in part 7.
Hindu Press-ups	3	8/8/8	A variety of a press up that you may not have come across before, please research correct form further if required, or refer to the demonstration.
Log Overhead Press (L)	3	8/8/10	Depending on the size and nature of the log, it may prove a challenge to get into the right position. Refer to the tutorial below. L = light log.
Log Bent-Over-Row (L)	3	8/8/10	You will need to attach handles made from rope. Please see part 7.

Conditioning and core

I am putting conditioning and core in a separate table just to make this distinction clear. You can either perform this ideally at the end of the upper body session or at a later point in the week on a separate day. Rest two minutes between each 'set', or round in this case when it comes to the interval-based conditioning.

Exercise	Sets	Duration	Notes
Plank	3	30 seconds	Make sure your hips stay level
Side Plank	3	30 seconds	Elbow in line with your shoulder joint
Plank Reach-outs	3	30 seconds	Plank position, but each arm is extended in front of the body alternately.
Tree Climbs	3	FT	FT = fastest time. Please refer to the tree climb explanation below
Tree Intervals	5	30 seconds	Sprint between two points in the woodland which are roughly 50 metres apart as many times as possible in 30 seconds
Cool down – go foraging			Refer to part 5

AMRAP to failure: Remember failure is until your form begins to break down. For example, on press-ups, you may no longer be able to lock out your arms fully. Remember to record all AMRAP's so that you are able to track your progress (a small journal may come in handy). The numbers will fluctuate over the coming weeks, depending on your current levels of energy or fatigue on that day. We are looking for an average increase over the course of the entire programme, so progress is clearly visible. It's not impossible that your press-up AMRAP will double during the entirety of the programme.

Pull-ups: It's very likely in moderately sized woodland you will be able to find a suitable branch from which to do pull-ups. Failing that, either utilise your rope or a spare towel or t-shirt you don't particularly care about. The rope option (depending on thickness) is extremely demanding of your grip and core strength. I will advocate these in the Oak programme. They will develop your grip strength to an even greater degree than regular pull-ups. If you get into the habit of doing this regularly, your grip will rival that of Hercules. This also applies to the towel or t-shirt option, however I find them less harsh on the hands. It is also possible to find a suitable length of wood, such as hazel, which is often straight to put between two branches of another tree and secure using your rope (you may need a knife to cut to size). Pull-ups are one of, if not the key movement of the Woodland Warrior programme. I perform them every day; nothing has built my upper body more.

Hindu Press-up: Start in the same position as you would a regular press-up. Now push your hips back as far as you can so your glutes are in the air and the balls of your feet are still on the ground. Moving in one fluid motion, push your hips back towards the ground and then push your torso upwards using your arms. Repeat for the desired number of repetitions.

Log Overhead Press: During my own experimentation whilst designing the Woodland Warrior programme, I found it consistently challenging to get heavier thick logs above my head. They lack the handles you see in commercially designed 'logs' for strongman training, however this does come with some benefits. Anything awkward and heavy which requires more stabilisation is going to ask more of your stabilising muscles and grip. If you're using a lighter log, it may be possible to simply grip and press overhead in one fluid motion.

Tree Climbs: Find a tree that is a reasonable height, no more than ten metres for your own safety. Some experimentation may be required and a decent search to find a tree that is suitable to climb in your chosen woodland. The objective will be to safely ascend and descend as quickly as possible either the entire tree or part of it. This doesn't necessarily mean climbing to the top of the tree and back down again. This could be climbing one particular sturdy branch, predominantly using the upper body. Similar to how you used 'monkey bars' as a child. I wouldn't expect the climb to last more than 10-30 seconds per attempt. This should contribute towards upper and lower body muscular endurance, hand to eye coordination, agility and dexterity, as well as grip strength. If needed, you can securely attach a rope to a sturdy branch in order to assist you. This exercise should also hopefully put you in the mind set of what it felt like to be one of your ancestors escaping a predator of a by-gone age or bring out your inner Tarzan. Either that or it will just prove to be a bit of fun conditioning.

Hawthorn lower body 1A weeks 1 & 2

Exercise	Sets	Reps	Notes
Log Squats (L)	3	15/12/10	Log needs to sit on the upper back/trapezius muscles
Log alternate lunges(L)	3	15/12/10	If you lose your balance at any point, stop and readjust.
Prisoner Squats (bodyweight)	3	20/20/10*	*5 second pauses at the bottom of the movement. Legs position held at 90 degrees.
Log Good Mornings (L)	3	12/12/12	Please see description
Log Romanian Deadlifts (L)	3	12/10/8	Please see description

Conditioning

Exercise	Sets	Reps	Notes
Plyo-Burpees	5	30 seconds	Please see description
Tree intervals	5	30 seconds	Sprint between two points in the woodland which are roughly 50 metres apart as many times as possible in 30 seconds

Plyo-Burpees: This exercise not only provides intensity for cardiovascular conditioning, but also adds mass to the lower body. Begin by entering a press-up position; from there you need to quickly bring your legs forward into a squatting position. As soon as your feet hit the ground, jump up as high as you can. Keep your arms by your sides. Land back on the balls of your feet and repeat.

Hawthorn upper 2B weeks 3 & 4

Exercise	Sets	Reps	Notes
Press-ups	3	8/10/AMRAP	Record AMRAP
Chin-ups	3	5/5/AMRAP	Record AMRAP
Log Dips	3	8/10/12	Please see description
Log Inverted Rows	3	8/10/12	Please see description
Log Overhead Press*(L/M)	3	8//8/6*	*Over-Head-Press. *You will now also need your medium log. For the last 3 reps of this set, lower the log back down to chest height for a slow count of 5.

Core and conditioning

Exercise	Sets	Reps	Notes
Plank	3	40 seconds	Make sure your hips stay level
Side plank	3	40 seconds	Elbow in line with your shoulder joint
Plank reach-outs	3	40 seconds	Just like the plank but each arm alternately reaches forward.

			Keep your core engage to stay balanced.
Tree climbs	4	FT	
Tree intervals	5	40 seconds	Sprint between two points in the woodland which are roughly 50 metres apart as many times as possible in 30 seconds.
Cool down – go foraging			Refer to chapter 6

Log Inverted Rows: Find a branch that allows you to tie two separate pieces of rope to create two loops that are shoulder width apart. Depending on the distance of your torso from the log and the log to the ground, you need to ensure they are long enough so you can perform a full range of motion. This movement focuses primarily on your upper back; this will help prevent imbalances from the large amount of vertical pulling you will be doing through pull-ups and chin-ups. I find it helpful to place one heel on the ground, followed by my other heel resting on top of that foot, then I lift my hips up. My arms are fully extended ready to bring my chest up towards the log, take a slight pause at the top then lower your torso for a slow count of three.

Hawthorn lower body 2B weeks 3 & 4

Exercise	Sets	Reps	Notes
Log Squats (L/M)	3	15/15/12*	*Last set of 12 is with the medium log.
Log Alternate Lunges	3	15/15/12*	*Last set of 12 is with the medium log.
Log Prisoner Squats (L)	3	15/15/12*	*5 second pauses at the bottom part of the movement
Log Good-Mornings (L)	3	10/10/12	
Log Romanian Deadlifts (M)	3	10/10/12	

Conditioning

Exercise	Sets	Reps	Notes
Plyo-Burpees	6	30 seconds	See description
Tree intervals	6	30 seconds	Sprint between two points in the woodland which are roughly 50

			metres apart as many times as possible in 30 seconds

Hopefully now that you have completed your first Woodland Warrior programme you have noticed some clear gains in both muscle size and strength. This won't be anything dramatic considering it's only been four or potentially eight weeks. But you should be able to provide evidence of an increase in the number of press-ups and pull-ups you can perform, the ease in which you can over-head press your L-Log, and the ease in which you can also squat both your L-Log and M-Log. Your recorded AMRAP's will now form your progression into the Hazel programme. If none of the above has been the case, repeat the Hawthorne programme and review your current recovery methods such as nutrition and sleep, as well as having an honest evaluation of the commitment and intensity you have brought to the workouts. As a rough guide, I would now expect you to be able to perform at least five pull-ups and ten press-ups with good form prior to starting the Hazel programme.

Some of the key concepts of the Woodland Warrior training system were introduced in the Hawthorn programme; therefore I won't explain them again. I will explain as much as possible any new movements or methods that are going to be introduced for the first time. This programme will be scheduled for four weeks, in blocks of two weeks, keeping the same frequency of four times a week. Two workouts for upper body and two workouts for lower body. If you feel it's needed, remember to follow the warmup routine mentioned prior to the Hawthorn programme.

Upper body workout 1C weeks 1 & 2

Exercise	Sets	Reps	Notes
Pull-ups	3	5/5/AMRAP*	See description
Log Overhead Press (L/M)	3	10/10/8	Last set of 8 is with your medium log
Log Land-Mine Press (L/M)	3	10/10/8	Last set of 8 is with your medium log. See description
Log Land-Mine Row (L/M)	3	10/10/8	Complete on both the right and left hand side of the body. See description
Press-ups	3	10/10/10*	*Last 5 repetitions, hold at 90 degrees for a 5 second count
Chin-ups	3	6/6/6	Perform these sets in a 3 minute time limit

Conditioning and core

Exercise	Sets	Reps	Notes
Log Carry Sprints (M)	5	30 Seconds	See description
Log Caber Toss (L)	5	FT	See description
Log Ab-Curl (L)	3	30 seconds	See description
Hanging Leg Raises	3	20 seconds	See description

Pull-up AMRAP: I want you to find the average of your pull-up ARMAP's over the duration of your time completing the Woodland Warrior programme so far. To work out the mean value (the average), add up the grand total of your pull-up AMRAP's and then divide by the total number of values. On this last set of pull-ups, you must at least match this number of repetitions.

Log Land-Mine Press: This exercise will isolate your deltoids to help you look like the thick oak tree you were born to be. If your light or medium log isn't particularly long and you cannot hinge one end of it either on the ground or against a tree trunk, then you will have to find a longer log of equal weight. Another alternative is to press the log while on your knees.

Complete this exercise on both the right and left shoulders for the same amount of repetitions. Holding one end of the log in your hand in line with your shoulder, press up until your arm is fully locked out.

Log Land-Mine Row: The same applies to this movement; you may have to find a longer log of equal weight. This movement will help isolate the back muscles on both the left and right hand side of the body. Holding one end of the log with your torso bent at a 90 degree angle, fully extend your arm then pull the log upwards so it is in line with your hip.

Log Carry Sprints: Nothing will quite combine both strength and conditioning like trying to carry a heavy object as fast as you can over a short distance. Get your medium log and place it on the floor. Make sure you have a roughly 50 metre clearing in the woodland that you can sprint across (Bonus points if it's on a slight incline). Begin by picking up your medium log and either hold it in your arms or balance it on your back or shoulder. Then sprint with it to the 50 metre line, drop and repeat. Do this as many times as possible in 30 seconds. You will most likely make it back to the starting position in this time. Rest for one minute then repeat.

Log Ab-Curl: This is a way to add some extra resistance to the traditional abdominal curl. Hold your light log in your arms and press. Now perform the abdominal crunch as you normally would. A lack of a full range of movement is the most common mistake I see when individuals perform an abdominal crunch, keep your torso straight, and make sure you perform a full ninety-degree movement.

Log Caber Toss: The caber toss has been a part of traditional highland games in Scotland since the 1800's. No wonder this country often produces such warriors of strength! Grab your medium log (the longer log used in the land mine movements may be a better choice). If you're in coniferous woodlands, with lots of pine or fir for example, a longer log that resembles those in the Highland Games may be easier to find. Lift the caber, grip it with clasped hands at the bottom and pivot. Balance the caber on your shoulder. As you begin to run to gain momentum, start off nice and slowly and then begin to speed up, when you get to what you think is your maximum speed, use your momentum and drive with your legs and hips while simultaneously pushing with your hands up towards your head and releasing the caber. Hopefully this has meant it has travelled some distance. You want to make sure that there aren't branches or other foliage above your head. Take your caber back to your starting point and repeat five times. Keep a good pace, and rest for no more than two minutes between each toss.

Hanging Leg Raises: This is a demanding core exercise for a number of reasons. As you will be hanging from your chosen pull-up branch or rope, there will be extra demand from your core in order to stabilise your body. Once you're stabilised, you have a choice of two variations, the latter being the more demanding option. The first variation allows you to keep your legs bent and you pull your knees up and towards your chest, then return to full extension. The second variation insists you keep your legs straight, and raise them directly in front of you, then lowering back to full extension whilst under control. Depending on your current ability, simply do as many repetitions as you can in the allotted time.

Hazel lower body 1C weeks 1 & 2

Exercise	Sets	Reps	Notes
Log Front Squats (L/M)	3	15/12/10*	See description. Last set of 10 with medium log
Jumping Lunges	3	12/12/12	You have 3 minutes to complete all 3 sets
Log Overhead Squats (L/M)	3	12/10/8*	See description. Use your medium log on the last set of 8
Jumping Squats	3	20 seconds	Make sure you really explode from the bottom of the movement. Ensure you keep your knees slightly soft for the landing

Conditioning (both solo and group options)

Exercise	Sets	Reps	Notes
Forest Exposure Run	1	20-30 minutes	See description
Murder Log			See description. You will need at least two people for this activity.

Log Front Squats: It is pretty much compulsory that the Woodland Warrior has tree trunks for legs. Nothing has added more mass to my quads quite like the front squat. It's also pretty demanding for the core. Your light and medium log will be cradled in your arms, similar to how a barbell is when a Zercher Squat is performed. I often take a slightly narrower stance when performing front squats and try to keep my torso as straight as possible during the movement.

Log Overhead Squats: Another squat variation that's going to ask even more of your core. Without a strong trunk, even the biggest of trees will fall in a storm. Get your log over your head in whatever way to wish, if it's the light log I would probably snatch it over-head. Or use your usual method to press the log over-head and balance it there. Engage the core as much as you can and keep constant tension in your arms. From here, squat down as low as you can and then return to the starting position.

Forest Exposure Run: Taking a break from the usual interval-based conditioning recommended in Woodland Warrior, this conditioning encourages you to simply jog or run, at a moderate pace through the woodland you have chosen as your training ground. This gives you an opportunity to focus on some of the positives we discovered in part 2, and possibly discover some of the wild edibles beyond your current training grove.

Murder Log: Be warned, this activity isn't for the faint hearted, and you will need to either be in a group or have a training partner. Find a relatively open area of the woodland, better yet an open pasture nearby. Split the group equally and separate an equal distance from each other. Mark out some kind of boundary using a log or whatever else you can find behind each team. Place the log or tree stump you have chosen in the centre of the battlefield, make sure this is a log that is medium in size and can be lifted by all those present. Provide some kind of count down and upon the go signal, each person or team has to race to the middle to retrieve the log and take it back over their boundary line. Expect tackling, wrestling, and headlocks to be the norm. Continue murder log for as long as you wish and keep score. Successful log retrieval equates to one point.

Hazel upper 2C weeks 3 & 4

Exercise	Sets	Reps	Notes
Log Overhead Press (M)	3	6/8/AMRAP	Record the number of repetitions for your AMRAP set
Log Up-Right Rows (L)	3	12/10/10	See description
Log Crucifix Hold	3	60 seconds	See description
Plyo-Press Ups	3	30 seconds	See description
Log Shrugs (M)	3	12/12/12	See description
Tree Pull-Ups	3	7/7/7	

Conditioning and core

Exercise	Sets	Reps	Notes
Tree Climbs	3	FT	Find the average time of your fastest tree climb attempts. At least match that time on your 3rd attempt.
Burpees	5	20 seconds	
Plank	3	40 seconds	
Lying Leg Raises	3	40 seconds	

Log Up-Right Row: This has always been one of favourite shoulder exercises. Some individuals complain of shoulder pain being increased by this movement, but as long as you bring the log just up to shoulder height, you should be absolutely fine. Tie two separate pieces of rope at equal distances on your light log to serve the purpose of handles. From that point, start with the log fully extended resting on the front of your hips or quads. From here, pull up the log and flare the elbows out to the sides until the log is perpendicular with your collar bone. Extend your arms back under control and repeat. If you are finding the light log too easy, try doing the exercise with your medium log. The aim is to constantly be challenging your body.

Log Crucifix Hold: This movement should have both of your shoulders begging to be released from their woodland nightmare. There is a reason that the crucifix hold is a common test of strength in strongman competitions. Find yourself two small logs, the kind that you would throw on the fire. Standing straight with your feet just over shoulder width apart, hold the two pieces of log fully extended for sixty seconds. Repeat three times.

Plyo-Press-Ups: Just like our trusted friend the regular press-up, you will probably be taken by surprise when you have a sick pump in your chest so extreme it's making the squirrels blush. With Plyo-Press-Ups, I want you to explode upwards on the movement as hard as you can in order to generate enough force that your hands come off the ground, even for just a split second. Add a clap if you feel like living on the edge. Don't rush this movement, just perform as many as you can in the time allocated. Focus on a safe landing and try to keep your elbows slightly soft in order to soften the impact.

Log Shrugs: While the emphasis of the Woodland Warrior won't ever be on isolation movements, having well developed trapezius muscles can make the difference between having what appears to be a 'pretty' physique and a powerful physique. Nothing portrays strength more in my opinion than slabs of muscle either side of your head. Find a second medium log if you haven't already, using handles you've created previously, tie a third piece of rope so they join. Holding each log either side of you with arms extended dip your chin down towards your chest, focus on pulling your trap muscles up towards your ears. Try to feel a stretch at the bottom part of the movement and take all the tension out of your arms. Or use your heavy log with two handles attached, refer to part 7.

Hazel lower body 2C weeks 3 & 4

Exercises	Sets	Reps	Notes
Log Squats (M)	3	10/10/10	Superset with Log lunges. As soon as you have completed a set of squats, immediately do a set of lunges.
Log Lunges (L)	3	10/10/10	Superset with Log Squats. As soon as you have completed a set of lunges, immediately do a set of squats.
Log Romanian Deadlifts (M)	3	12/12/15	
Jumping Lunges	3	12/12/12	Superset with squat jumps
Jumping Squats	3	12/12/12	Superset with squat lunges

Plyo-Burpees	3	30 seconds	

Conditioning – perform as a circuit. Take two minutes rest after each set.

Exercise	Sets	Reps	Notes
Burpees	3	30 seconds	
Mountain Climbers	3	30 seconds	
Tuck Jumps	3	30 seconds	
High Knees	3	30 seconds	

The end of the Hazel programme

Just as with the Hawthorn programme, if you wish to repeat this programme for eight weeks, please do so. Keep the record of your AMRAP's as these will inform some of your training in the final Oak programme. The Oak programme will have a significant increase in volume and introduce new exercises, while keeping the key log compound movements you have now come to expect. Make sure you can clearly see some progression in the number of repetitions for key movements like press-ups, pull-ups, and over-head press before beginning. If you can't by this stage perform at least eight to ten pull-ups, then do not move on to the Oak programme. You should also be averaging at least twenty or more press-ups. The oak programme will also be introducing movements that isolate certain muscle groups. The expectation to train four times a week with an upper and lower split will remain. However, conditioning and core will be advised for separate training days where possible. Therefore your training week may look something this this:

Week Day	Workout
Monday	Upper
Tuesday	Conditioning and Core
Wednesday	Lower
Thursday	Conditioning
Friday	Upper
Saturday	Rest day
Sunday	Lower + Conditioning and core

How you split your training week isn't gospel, as mentioned previously. Consistency is still of paramount importance, so complete what is necessary when you can. It will be designed as the pinnacle of the Woodland Warrior method, which can be repeated indefinitely with added progressions from consistently reviewing your progress and adjusting intensity variables accordingly. The Oak Programme is designed to be repeated twice.

The Oak Programme

Oak upper body 1D weeks 1 & 2

Exercises	Sets	Reps	Notes
Pull-ups	4	8/8/8/8*	*On the last set of 8, lower yourself for a slow count of 3 on every rep
Tarzan Pull-ups	4	6/6//6/6	See description
Log Overhead Press (M/H)	4	8/8/8/3*	*You will need your heavy log for this last set. Remember to use the Steinborn Method to get the log on your back ready to over-head press. Do so behind the neck if need be. If the log falls on the descent, repeat to simply make it 3 separate repetitions.
Log Crucifix Hold	4	60 seconds	Remember to use smaller logs of equal size
Decline Press-Ups	4	12/12/12	Prop your feet on to another tree stump or log
Press-ups	4	12/12/AMRAP	Remember to record your AMRAP
Log Deadlifts (M/H)	4	10/10/8/8	See description. Last two sets of 8 are with the heavy log
Log Bent-Over Rows (M/H)	4	10/10/6/6	Last 2 sets of 6 are with the heavy log
Log Bicep Curls (L)	4	15/12/12	See description
Log Overhead Tricep Extensions (L)	4	15/12/12	See description
Log Shrugs (H)	4	15/15/15/15	

Conditioning and core

Exercise	Sets	Reps	Notes
Log Farmer Walks (2 x H)	5	60 seconds	*see description
Caber Toss (H)	5	60 seconds	
Log Sit-Ups	4	40 seconds	

Plank	3	80 seconds	

Tarzan Pull-ups: Who doesn't want to look like an even juicier version of the archetypical Woodland Warrior, Tarzan? To perform this pull-up variation, grip the middle of the branch with both hands close together. Exhale and pull yourself up and as you reach the top, pull your body to the right before lowering and then repeating but this time to the left side.

Log Deadlifts: You're probably wondering why the deadlift hasn't made an appearance already, other than in its Romanian form, which is designed to mostly target the lower back and hamstrings. With a log rather than a barbell does make it a bit more awkward to perform, as I guess is the case with a lot of these movements. Once again, tie two separate loops around your heavy log about shoulder width apart. Make sure their length allows you to have your legs slightly bent and not straight as we would in the Romanian Deadlift. Grab the log (or handles) legs shoulder width apart and toes pointing slightly outwards. Dip your hips and engage your lateral muscles. Do this by making sure you're holding the rope as tight as you can and allowing no space between your arms and arm pits. To initiate the lift, imagine you're pushing the forest floor away from you. As the log begins to travel pass your knees, push your hips forward to reach full lock out. I would strongly recommend everyone knows how to perform a barbell deadlift correctly before attempting the log deadlift. Please complete further research online or with other experienced strength athletes. I am under no illusion that a log isn't the best method to perform what many people consider to be the king of exercises.

Log Bicep Curls: While it's my belief that both your biceps and triceps would have already experienced hypotrophy from the current upper body movements, I don't think any harm will come in providing them with some extra added mass. A decent arm measurement for a natural lifter is anything around seventeen inches. Using your light log and your tightest grip, stand up straight and glue your elbows to your sides. Lower the log at a controlled pace until your arms are fully extended. Bring back up under a controlled pace and continue. This movement will also provide hypertrophy for your forearms.

Log Overhead Tricep Extensions: I prefer a large tree stump or some kind of wood mass different from a log for this exercise. An elongated log may not work quite as well but it's still doable (perhaps use a light or medium log that already has rope handles). Begin by extending the wood above your head using whatever grip gives you the best hold. From here, bend the elbows 90 degrees behind your head and then return to the starting position and repeat.

Log Farmers Walk: Not only will this exercise increase your level of conditioning, but it should also help towards having traps that need their own postcode and a grip that could crush any log. Using the same rope handles as you do for shrugs, simply carry both your heavy logs (if you haven't already, find yourself a second heavy log) and walk a maximum distance for one minute. If you have limited space, walk in a straight line and turn around.

Oak lower body 1D weeks 1 & 2

Exercise	Sets	Reps	Notes
Log Squats (M/H)	4	12/11/AMRAP*	The final AMRAP set is with your heavy log
Log Lunges (M/H)	4	12/11/6*	Last set is with your heavy log
Log Prisoner Squats (M)	4	12/12/12	
Plyo-burpees	4	30 seconds	Superset with Jumping Lunges
Jumping Lunges	4	30 seconds	Superset with Plyo-Burpees
Tree Sit	1	Longest Time	With your back up against a tree, lower yourself into a seated position, legs at 90 degrees. Place a light log on your lap with your hands out in front. Record your time in order to beat at a later stage.

Conditioning

Exercise	Sets	Reps	Notes
Hill Sprints	7	10-15 seconds	Find some woodland or nearby hill. The sprint up the hill should take you between 10-15 seconds. Repeat 7 times.
Cool-down - Foraging			See Chapter 5

Oak upper body workout 2D weeks 3 & 4

Exercise	Sets	Reps	Notes
Rope Pull-Ups	3	5/5/5	Make sure your rope is attached to a sturdy branch. If it's thin, best to double up. Make sure each handle is at equal lengths.
Pull-ups	4	8/8/ AMRAP	On the last set, try to match or exceed your current average AMRAP on pull-ups.
Log Overhead Press (M/H)	4	8/8/8/AMRAP*	Use your heavy log with the last set. If you are

			repeating the Oak programme twice, try to match or exceed your current AMRAP.
Log Land-Mine Press (M/H)	4	10/8/8/6*	Remember this movement is with each arm. Try to use your heavy log on the last set. Kneel down if required.
Hand Stand Press-ups	3	3/3/3	If you're unable to complete this movement, then perform 2 x Press Up AMRAP of 60 seconds.
Diamond Press-ups	4	15/15/15/15	
Log Shrugs (H)	4	15/15/20/20	
Log Deadlifts (M/H)	4	10/10/10/8*	*Last set of 8 uses your heavy log.
Log Bicep Curl	4	15/15/15/AMRAP	
Log Overhead Tricep Extensions	4	15/15/15/AMRAP	

Conditioning and core – complete as a circuit. Take two minutes rest between each.

Exercise	Sets	Reps	Notes
Jump-ins	1	4	
Bicycle Crunches	1	4	
Burpees	1	4	
Toe Touches	1	4	
Optional: Murder Log	20 -30 minutes		
Optional: Log of War	20-30 minutes		See description

Log of War: This is an optional group activity. Find a long and sturdy log. You will need at least two people; the more people taking part, the longer the log required. The log is basically taking the place of a rope in traditional tug of war. Set a centre line, using some rope or another log. The first team to pull the entirety of the log over the centre line wins. Play several rounds to declare the Log of War champions.

Oak lower body 2D weeks 3 & 4

Exercise	Sets	Reps	Notes
Log Front Squats (M/H)	4	12/12/10/AMRAP*	Heavy log is used for the AMRAP set
Log Farmers Walk (2 x H)	6	60 seconds	
Tree sit	3	60 seconds	
Log Lunges (H)	4	8/8/6/6	
Log Squats	4	10/10/5/5*	Last 2 sets of 5 are with your heavy log

Conditioning

Exercise	Sets	Reps	Notes
Tree Climbs	4	FT	
Caber Toss	6	60	

Below I will outline some circuits designed as a one-off workout or at periods when you really want to claim the forest as your own.

The Major Oak

The Major Oak is a large English oak near the village of Edwinstowe in north Nottinghamshire within Sherwood Forest. It is thought to be at least 1000 years old. Legend has it that the ancient oak was used by Robin Hood and is the location where he and his merry men slept.

In honour of this tree and its existence in England for a millennium, perform the following as a circuit. There is no time limit and you can use a log of your choice. Repeat this three times, and then choose one of the exercises to perform for one final set of 10 x 10 to take the total number of repetitions to 1000.

Exercise	Sets	Reps	Note
Log Overhead Press	10	10	100 reps in total
Tree Pull-ups	10	10	100 reps in total
Log Squats	10	10	100 reps in total

The Llangernyw Yew

The Llangernyw Yew is an ancient tree growing in Conwy, Wales. It is estimated to be between 4000 and 5000 years old. This would date the tree to at least the Bronze Age. This makes the Llangernyw a candidate for the oldest still standing tree in Great Britain. Local folklore suggests that its cleft trunk serves as a portal to the world of the dead; it is located in the centre of a cemetery after all.

In honour of the Llangeryw Yew, perform the circuit below with a 40 minute time limit and try to complete as many sets and repetitions as possible. You may choose to rest for two minutes between each circuit. (AMSAP = as many sets as possible)

Exercise	Sets	Reps	Notes
Rope Pull-ups	AMSAP	5	
Caber Toss	AMSAP	5	Throw the caber as far as you can. Run to its landing spot, and then toss again. Repeat 5 times.
Log Overhead Press	AMSAP	5	
Log Bent Over Rows	AMSAP	5	
Press-ups	AMSAP	5	
Log Front Squats	AMSAP	5	

The Druid Warrior

Inspired by the barbaric rites of the Druids that once roamed the ancient forest groves, this will truly test your worth as a Woodland Warrior. Complete this circuit as many times as possible in one hour. It must be performed as close as possible to an oak tree. Post circuit you must forage at least three wild edible plants or fungi and consume as your post workout woodland feast.

Exercise	Set	Reps	Notes
Tree Pull-Ups	AMSAP	8	
Log Squats	AMSAP	8	
Log Overhead Press	AMSAP	8	
Log Deadlifts	AMSAP	8	
Diamond Pres-Ups	AMSAP	8	
Log Sit-Ups	AMSAP	8	
Log Curls	AMSAP	8	
Log Lunges	AMSAP	8	
Log Overhead Tricep Extensions	AMSAP	8	
Log Crucifix Hold	AMSAP	2 minutes	
Tree Sits	AMSAP	3 minutes	

The end of the Oak programme

Congratulations if you've made it this far. Consider yourself a Woodland Warrior. The scent of pine and deciduous detritus should be constantly upon your skin.

The ease at which you perform pull-ups and place an enormous log upon your well-developed traps should turn the heads of all fellow woodland creatures.

You can continue to follow the Woodland Warrior programme indefinitely if you wish. Remember to adapt and find new logs when required if they become too easy or no longer fit the definitions of the light, medium, and heavy logs I outlined at the beginning. Constantly record your AMRAPs and find the average. Always try to match or beat these throughout the programme when you believe it is justified.

Each stage of the Woodland Warrior programme would benefit to be repeated twice. Don't worry if you hit a plateau and no new AMRAPs are set for some time. This eventually occurs for us all in certain movements. Sooner or later an extra rep or two will emerge from the foundations of the forest. Don't be afraid to mix and match certain elements from each programme, or to adjust what is required for your own personal circumstances.

As you will see, some workouts included foraging as your cool down. This is a chance to explore the woodland and surrounding environment for wild edible and fungi post workout which is a crucial part of the overall Woodland Warrior training system.

"In the science of ecology, one learns that a human being is not an organism in an environment, but is an organism-environment; that is to say; a unified field of behaviour" – Alan Watts

Even in the twenty-first century, a large proportion of Britain and other parts of the world are covered by many edible wild plants and fungi. It is my opinion that foraging has numerous benefits for us all, and certainly enough to constitute a whole book, of which there are already many.

In woodlands, pastures, parks, hedgerows, and on the coast, there are flowers, leaves, nuts, berries and fungi that will quite easily rival the most well-known commercially available 'superfoods'. For example, stinging nettles alone contain 269mg per 100g of vitamin C compared to the humble orange at just 53mg of vitamin C per 100g. A hazelnut contains more protein pound for pound than a hen's egg. Many plants we commonly considered to be weeds were once cultivated and used by the most ancient of civilisations.

Through a loss of knowledge and changes in culinary fashion, their use and flavour has been all but forgotten. A forager, or in this case a Woodland Warrior, can have a diet almost unknown to the zombified supermarket shopper.

You will never be closer to nature than when you are gathering from the bosom of its bounty. I feel an almost unrivalled symbiosis with it when I'm foraging. It's like an innate form of communication is created the more time I spend foraging in my local environment. I'm learning a language that only I and the surrounding biodiversity understand. As someone who isn't spiritual by nature, foraging has provided me with some of the few experiences I would consider to be spiritual in any regard.

Pick a hazelnut, eat a blackberry, or roast the roots of a burdock, and you are engaging in the same behaviours as our prehistoric ancestors. They thrived on such foods, and so can you. You will never forget the intrinsic satisfaction that comes from taking home and preparing your first wild food. The seasonal clock will dictate what you gather, just as it ruled the lives of our ancestors. Time will have an importance once more beyond the nihilistic factory bells introduced over the past 200 years. You will become so familiar with your local natural ecosystem that where you live will take on an entirely new meaning.

The modern world often views practices such as foraging as an absurd affectation at best. The pursuit of hipsters, or something that only middle-class hippies from Glastonbury choose to do. When we forage, we truly know what we are eating, and we feel that we actually deserve the food we have found. In this sense, we live very unnatural lives nowadays because we source much of our food in the local supermarket. I wouldn't be surprised that from this point forward you feel more human inside of the woods than outside of it.

With time you will become trained to spot even the most subtle of wild edibles from the corner of your eye. A cornucopia of tasty treats will greet you rather than a carpet of green. I call this 'the forager's eye'. You will unlock a long-lost skill which sits locked behind a lifetime of modernity.

In this part of the Woodland Warrior I will first outline some practical precautions that need to be kept in mind while foraging. I will introduce three wild edibles from each season that I believe are the easiest and most prolific to find, as well as highlighting their benefits for the purpose of this training programme. A recipe of some kind will accompany each wild food pick, but I am in no way a talented or even competent cook, so simply recommend the way I often consume them. This information will just be a small fragment of the true extent of foraging. I hope it inspires you to learn as much as you possibly can about the topic and attend foraging workshops.

If you're wondering why I haven't included any kind advocating for hunting the wild game of the woodland, I felt this would have created an ethical quagmire that would have been difficult to navigate. The humane and effective hunting of wildlife such as deer and rabbit can take decades to master, any advice or instruction I could have given within this document would not do this task any justice.

The nutrition of building muscle

I believe nutrition can be overcomplicated for the recreational lifter. I'm not saying that the science of nutrition isn't of huge importance, or something that doesn't take years to master, but when it comes to those who compete in bodybuilding or strength sports, these nutritional recommendations need to be extremely specific. I write the below assuming that this doesn't apply to the large majority reading Woodland Warrior.

If you're trying to build muscle, you will need a surplus of calories. No matter how hard you train, the process of creating new muscle tissue won't be optimised if you do not provide the body with enough energy to do so. I am an advocate of tracking your calories and macros. Many apps are available that make this tedious task just that much easier. In order to establish how many calories you are going to need, multiply your current bodyweight in pounds by 14 and 17. The middle value between these two multiplications is a rough estimate of the calories you require to maintain your current bodyweight.

To gain weight, add a surplus of anywhere between 200 to 400 calories, and aim for around 0.2 kg of bodyweight gained per week. To lose weight, reduce your maintenance calories by approximately 200 to 400 calories and aim for 0.2kg of weight loss per week.

When it comes to macronutrients (which is the amount of protein, carbohydrates, and fats required to assist muscle building) you will want to aim for 0.7-1g of protein per pound of bodyweight. Carbohydrates will need to be approximately 2-3g per pound of bodyweight, and fats 0.5g per pound of bodyweight. These are the macros I would advise if you want to maximise lean muscle gain. Monitoring macronutrients is of less importance than calories. If you stick to lean sources of protein, high fibrous vegetables, unprocessed sources of carbohydrates like potatoes, sweet potatoes and both brown and white rice, then you should achieve basic optimisation of your nutritional intake. To continue to maximise your nutrition beyond this point, the wild edibles recommended will be an excellent inclusion.

One maxim that has always served me incredibly well is the following; the less that's been done to that particular food, the better. It is a good idea to consume smaller and more regular portions throughout the day. Supplements such as protein powder do have their place in helping you fulfil the demand for protein, but they aren't absolutely essential. Everybody has a slightly different metabolic rate, and experiences different effects to macronutrients such as carbohydrates. The caloric intake and food selection which best suits your individual needs will take time and experimentation to discover. An intake of foods dense in vitamins and essential minerals is also highly important, not only for building muscle but also for optimal health. This will help keep a hormonal profile in the body that will increase your chances of success.

Precautions

I will first of all focus on the laws that will affect your foraging if you are based in Great Britain. If you are based anywhere else, please become familiar with your own local laws surrounding the gathering of wild plants and fungi.

When it comes to accessing private property, the law works slightly differently in Scotland when compared to England and Wales. The Scottish Land Reform Act 2003 allows anyone to access any piece of land, as long as they do so responsibly. This has been a long held tradition in Scotland, which has only recently been made into law. So as long as you don't camp in someone else back garden, or chase the local wild life around naked with just a spear in your hand, then you can pretty much go wondering where you please. Whether you think this notion sounds like a good idea or not most likely depends on your perspective.

In England and Wales the large proportion of countryside available is under private ownership, therefore if you do not have permission to access or aren't following the public footpaths, then you can be accused of trespassing. I wouldn't object for a second anyone wishing to enter my property for any of the purposes I've outlined within Woodland Warrior. And if everyone treated nature and the countryside with as much respect as those reading this book no doubt do, then a policy similar to that of Scotland may be possible in England one day. However, after my family have dealt with fly tipping, littering, poaching, dogging, and theft for decades, I have my doubts as to whether such freedom of access would work and benefit the countryside overall. I do believe that the large majority of landowners will permit you access, as long as you treat their land with respect.

All this being said, public access forests and national parks do exist, as well as many outdoor spaces under the ownership of public bodies like the National Trust. It is not illegal for you to forage fungi. Some are considered of special scientific interest, and rightfully so, and therefore shouldn't be picked. But none of these will be included in this part of the programme. The Countryside Act of 1981 prohibits the up-rooting of any plant on private property, and you should carry a knife with you no longer than 3 inches nor should it have a fixed blade.

The farmer and his or her shotgun is probably the least of your worries when it comes to foraging. While some fungi for example can be an absolute delight to eat, others such as the Death Cap can leave you in a heap of agony on the forest floor as it slowly destroys your vital organs. Six months later, as the frozen hand of your corpse emerges from a fine blanket of snow, you make the national news after the local dog walker has to pull her pug away to stop nibbling on your left index finger.

Identification is absolutely vital. I always check anything I find across multiple resources, both books and fellow foragers. If you're in any doubt whatsoever, do not eat it. Please read that twice. This applies to both fungi and plants. I will clearly outline if any of the wild edibles I recommend have any poisonous imposters to be aware of. It is always a good idea to initially have a small amount of what you've gathered if it is the first time you are consuming it. Some individuals can have allergic reactions to a number of otherwise perfectly edible plants. When it comes to where you collect your wild edibles, just avoid busy road sides or pathways that have a high level of human traffic.

In terms of what you will need foraging, avoid taking a plastic carrier bag. Use a basket (if you can make a basket look masculine, you've reached full Woodland Warrior status) of a wicker variety. This is far better for the preservation of the fungi and plants, but it also allows the mushroom spores to be potentially dispersed to reproduce on your journey home. I prefer to cut the stem of the mushroom just up from the base, so a knife comes in handy. I also like to use mesh storage bags for both plants and fungi. Equipment wise, I think that will suffice. Always forage responsibly and never take more than what you need. Don't get too adventurous too soon; it's better to know and use a few wild edibles well than to try to be an amateur botanist and end up spending half the night awake with stomach cramps.

Spring

I often find spring to be the best time for plants when it comes to foraging. Most mushrooms have yet to awaken from their winter slumber and lay in waiting for the damp conditions of autumn. Spring, which I consider to be from March to May, is when Mother Nature puts on the greenest of her capes. You'll soon discover plants and fungi don't read the same books as we do, and both will sometimes or quite often appear out of season, as well as some being available for most of the year. Spring is a time when we take advantage of the fresh and sweet tasting wild plants and the nutrient dense young shoots.

Stinging Nettle (Urtica Dioica) March – July

Many people are surprised to discover that such a prolific weed, which is considered to be a painful burden on their otherwise tranquil walks, is in actual fact one of the most nutritious plants known to man.

This plant has a long and rich history of human consumption and use. Evidence of nettles being consumed dates back over 8000 years. Nettle dumplings are considered to be one of Britain's oldest known dishes. Neolithic chefs would mix nettle leaves with other wild edibles, barley and flour to create these dumplings. Nettle distribution is often a key marker of human habitation.

Nettle hasn't only been utilised as a source of food, but also fabric. Nettle fibre use dates back to the Bronze Age. Up until the 18th century, it was regularly used to make garments in the Scottish highlands. During the First World War, German uniforms were up to 85% nettle fibre.

The stings of the nettle are caused by tiny hypodermic needles that inject formic acid into the body. Roman Soldiers during their first invasions of the British Isles were known to whip themselves with nettles to help stay warm during winter campaigns as it is known to increase blood flow throughout the body.

The plant itself is almost too well known to need describing. If you're unsure for even a second, try touching it. There is a method to take leaves straight from the plant without getting stung. The skin on the end of your fingertips is normally more tolerant, pick from the freshest leaves at the top of the plant. Pinch your thumb and forefinger together then grab the leaf at the base and pull. Fold the leaf in on itself into a small parcel, and then pop it straight in your mouth. You can pick nettles all the way up until July; at this point the plant begins to experience a build-up of calcium oxalate crystals that can irritate the kidneys. There is normally a second re-growth later on in the year, just avoid plants with long dropping seed heads.

Stinging nettles are incredibly high in protein. Anywhere between 30%-40% of their dry mass constitutes this essential micronutrient for building muscle. From 100g of nettle, this would equate to anywhere up to 40g of protein.

It's absolutely packed full of A and C vitamins, as well as some B vitamins. Per 100g it contains 670mg of potassium, 590mg of calcium, 86mg of magnesium and 4.4mg of iron.

Iron can be found in every cell of the body. It transports oxygen in the blood to the tissues, allowing our muscles to work effectively. Post-workout, it will help produce new cells, proteins, and hormones. Iron will help you not only move actual iron, but timber too.

Some studies have suggested nettles can also help maintain optimal production of testosterone, a key hormone when it comes to adding muscle mass.

If you're not already utilising nettle power, now is the time to start.

Nettle Soup Recipe

The easiest way I find to consume nettles is either straight from the plant, boiled in some water to make a tea, or as a soup, the recipe of which I'll include below. This recipe is very basic; you can add more ingredients to make it more of a delicacy if you want.

Ingredients: 300g of nettle leaves, 70g unsalted butter, 1 medium onion chopped, 1 large potato chopped, 2 gloves of garlic chopped, 2 litres of vegetable stock.

Method: Melt the butter in a hot pan and add the onions and garlic allowing this to simmer for 5 minutes. Add the potato and continue to cook until soft. Add the nettles and vegetable stock and simmer for a further 5 minutes. Allow to cool slightly, then puree by whatever method you wish. Reheat and enjoy.

Garlic Mustard (Alliaria Petiolata) March – May

You will likely find garlic mustard on the edges of your chosen woodland. It's prolific, and shouldn't take much considerable effort to find. It also goes by the name of 'beggar man's oatmeal', suggesting that it was probably used to a large degree during times of famine. Despite its availability, it has attracted little folklore or historical documentation.

It will emerge in early spring, bearing light green leaves and later clusters of white flowers. It will have heart shaped, or kidney shaped leaves, depending upon your perspective. The easiest way to identify this plant is to crush such leaves in between your fingers; a strong but not overwhelming smell of garlic should greet your nostrils.

The leaves are best when picked prior to the plant flowering, but they are still edible when flowers have emerged. The flower heads themselves are also edible, however they produce a far more intense and almost bitter garlic taste. They make a good addition to any salad, and can be combined with other wild edibles like hawthorn and common sorrel. Common sorrel will be described in detail in the section on summer, hawthorn will be utilised in the autumn.

It's a member of the mustard family, which includes cabbages and cauliflower. It has been proven to contain the cancer preventing chemicals isothio-cyanates. It also contains allyl sulfides, known to combat tumour proliferation.

Garlic mustard greens have substantial amounts of vitamins A, C, E and some of the B vitamins. In addition, this wild weed contains potassium, calcium, magnesium, selenium, copper, iron and manganese as well as omega-3 fatty acids.

Magnesium is an essential mineral that plays a critical role in the human body. It takes part in the process of energy metabolism and assists the maintenance of normal muscle function.

Use both your eyes and your sense of smell next time you are in the woodland to discover garlic mustard.

Recipe – Garlic Mustard Pesto

Besides adding it to salads, soups, or simply in your choice of sandwich, you could make some pesto to accompany your whole-wheat pasta and lean choice of protein.

Ingredients: 100g Garlic Mustard leaves, 1 clove garlic, 50g pine nuts, 5 gherkins, 50g grated Parmesan, 10tbsp oil, salt and pepper.

Method: Wash, shake, and roughly chop the leaves. Put them in the blender with the garlic, pine nuts, gherkins and then mix until a smooth paste is achieved. Add the Parmesan, oil, a pinch of salt, and a dash of pepper then blend quickly for the final time.

Dryads Saddle (Polyporus squamosus) April – May

Mushrooms always fill me with more excitement than plants. Maybe it's the slightly riskier task of their identification, or the fact they are often surrounded in a rich mythos. Come autumn, they truly dominate many woodlands as the edible of choice. In spring, they are few and far between, especially in the depths of the forest. But the Dryads Saddle should be a frequent encounter on your hunt for more logs.

This mushroom gets its name from ancient Greek mythology. A dryad was a woodland spirit or nymph, and legend has it they would use this mushroom as a saddle on their journey through the woodlands. No doubt in search of some Woodland Warriors to torment.

Often found growing on fallen deciduous trees, this mushroom proves easy to identify. You will find no real lookalikes at this time of year. It also goes by the name of the pheasant back fungus, due to its unique 'scales' on the cap surface that resemble that of a female hen bird. It's the largest cap mushroom in the UK, growing up to 60cm in diameter. The pores underneath the cap resemble a honey comb. Some say it has the unmistakable scent of watermelon, but once cooked it has a mild woody mushroom taste.

The mushroom is at its best while it is still young, and around 10-20cm in diameter. As it ages, apart from the likelihood of maggot infestation, it becomes leathery and unpalatable. Sometimes the outer inches of the cap can still be worthy of foraging, simply cut this off with your knife. This mushroom likes a combination of warm and wet weather, so if we have some early spring sunshine followed by showers it will be more likely to make an appearance.

You will get both medicinal and nutritional benefits directly from the woodland when you consume Dryads Saddle. It has well researched immunomodulatory properties, helping sustain a well-functioning immune system. It also contains Lectin, a carbohydrate binding protein which helps to prevent the death of new and productive cells. It's comprised of approximately 65% carbohydrates, 15% protein (which is pretty good for fungi) and 3% fat.

Recipe – Shallow Fried Dyad Saddle

Ingredients: 400g Dryad Saddle, 2 spoons of white flour, 2 eggs, Salt and Pepper, Vegetable oil.

Method: Slice the mushroom into thick pieces. Make sure you're using relatively young mushrooms and put any form of stalk to one side. Mix the flour, salt, and pepper to taste. Throw in some extra spices or herbs if you want. Dust the mushrooms with the flour and then coat with the beaten egg. The oil should be roughly half the thickness of the slices of mushroom. Cook for 3 minutes each side. Serve as a compliment to whatever main meal you have planned.

Summer

As spring comes to an end, you will probably notice that many edible plants are no longer available. I always find that there is often an awkward time between seasons with some wild edibles becoming far less prevalent. And I often find it most noticeable between spring and summer, from the beginning of June onwards. Plants obey the climate more than the seasons so it's likely you will find some of the wild edibles of spring still available in the early summer.

However, all is not lost for the Woodland Warrior in summer. Not only do you welcome the summer solstice and the increased amount of sun, there are still some performance enhancing wild treats waiting to be found.

Yarrow (Achillea Millefolium) May – November

Yarrow has a rich history of use in herbal medicine throughout the ages. From the Ancient Greeks to the Anglo-Saxons, from the southern coasts, to the highlands of Scotland, its applications have been well documented.

Yarrow has always been valued as an astringent plant that helps cease bleeding from scratches, cuts, wounds and sores. The Romans considered it so effective at this task it was named Herba Militaris due to its wide spread use during military campaigns.

The Ancient Greeks consider yarrow to be the plant that the great Achilles used to bind the wounds of his soldiers at Troy, hence the first part of its Latin name. The second part refers to its crowded foliage, 'milfoil' meaning 'thousand leaves'.

The Celts were convinced that consumption of the yarrow plant allowed you to have visions of your future spouse emerging from the woodland or meadow.

Yarrow tea is thought to be a detoxifier, cleansing the skin and purifying the blood of any unfortunate soul stricken with sickness or disease.

Both the leaves and flowers can be eaten. The leaves can be added to any salad, soup, or simmered in butter like any green vegetable. You will most likely find yarrow in any pasture surrounding woodland. It can reach up to 60 cm in height and will eventually have a white flower head. The leaves will be elongated with almost brush like in appearance.

Various studies have demonstrated yarrow has anti-anxiety effects, of both a short and long term nature. It can mimic the effects of Valium, increasing the quality of the sleep and reducing feelings of depression. Yarrow can lower markers of stress and therefore the production of cortisol. High levels of cortisol in the body can have detrimental effects on the ability of your body to recover from any strenuous activity.

Recipe - Yarrow Tea

Yarrow flowers, leaves and stems can be used to make a medicinal tea. You can use either the fresh or dried flower or leaves. Yarrow tea can taste bitter so you can use honey to take the edge off if needed.

Ingredients: 3 fresh yarrow leafs, 1 cup boiling water, 1 teaspoon honey (optional), 1 lemon slice (optional)

Method: Steep the yarrow leaves in boiling water for 10 minutes. Remove the leaves if desired. Add honey and/or lemon juice if needed.

Common Sorrel (Rumex Acetosa) March – September

As the name suggests, common sorrel is a particularly abundant plant. It is found in the pastures surrounding woodland, particularly those that haven't experienced a large amount of recent agricultural activity. It is available for most of the year, but it becomes slightly more elusive at the height of summer.

As a garden and medicinal herb, it has recorded use by Rome's Pliny the Elder, during the 1st Century AD.

Common sorrel consumption was at its most prevalent during the reign of King Henry VIII. Its arrow-shaped leaves were a familiar sight in medieval vegetable gardens across Europe well into the 1700s.

The dark speared shaped leaves are reminiscent of Docks, from which this plant shares a genus. It grows anywhere between 2cm -25cm tall. The young leaves are the most tender and tasty, with a distinctive taste of apple peel. Always check that the end of the leaves are pointed and not curved, in order to avoid confusion with the young lords and ladies plant.

Sorrel contains very high amounts of vitamin C; just 75g of fresh sorrel leaves will provide you with over half of your daily recommended allowance. It also contains beta-carotene, which has been shown to help preserve the health and strength of the lungs, increasing the amount of air one can breathe in a single breath. This increased lung capacity might come in handy when you need to perform hill sprints or if you're trying to win a game of murder log.

Recipe – Medieval Sorrel Soup

We now visit our second soup, something that's also quite simple to make next to your campfire. Put on your best crown and marry at least eight women to fully appreciate this medieval delicacy.

Ingredients: 30 sorrel leaves, 1 medium potato, 1 medium onion, 25g butter, 1.2 litres of chicken stock, salt and black pepper.

Method: Wash the Sorrel leaves, chop the onion and slice the potato. Melt the butter and fry the onion until it softens. Add the potato and continue cooking for a few more minutes. Put in the sorrel leaves and cook until they appear to wilt. Now add the chicken stock and cook on a low heat until the potato appears to soften. Blend using your chosen method (possibly not an option if you've chosen to make it whilst out camping) season and serve.

Field Mushroom (Agaricus campestris) July – October

We now encounter our second mushroom recommended for the Woodland Warrior, the field mushroom. This fungus is likely to be found in the surrounding fields and pastures of any woodland, especially in paddocks that are used by livestock. You may also find this at the side of country lanes or on the edges of woodland paths. The wood mushroom, Agaricus silvicola, is incredibly similar and will also appear in woodland from September onwards.

These mushrooms are best collected in the early morning as they often emerge overnight. You're in a race with other Woodland Warriors to collect them before they are gone, but thankfully they often appear in abundance.

The field mushroom is often one of the first mushrooms that comes to anyone's attention. Strolling through your local fields, you've probably already glanced at one and thought how similar it looked to the very ones you buy in the supermarket. Most edible mushrooms that you can buy are a cultivated version of the agarics, a rather large family of mushrooms. This resemblance should only partially inform your identification.

You're looking for a white domed cap, flattening out with age. The gills should be crowded, they first appear dark pink turning to dark brown. The flesh should be white, bruising slightly pink when cut. If it rapidly turns a vivid yellow and has a very chemical like smell, this may mean it's the *Agaricus xanthodermus*, which is mildly poisonous. The confusion between these two species is one of the biggest causes of mushroom poisoning. The Yellow Stainer won't kill you, but it will certainly leave you stuck to the toilet for some time.

Sharing the common benefits of all mushroom consumption, the field mushroom contains vitamin B3 and B5. A lack of B vitamins is associated with a reduced high-intensity exercise performance. Something which is of great importance for the duration of the Woodland Warrior programme.

Recipe – Field Mushroom Omelette

This recipe will also work with all mushrooms mentioned so far apart from the wood ear mushroom (winter).

Ingredients: 3 field mushrooms, butter, 3 eggs, cheese (optional), salt and pepper.

Method: Chop up the field mushrooms, avoid washing directly, just get rid of any obvious dirt. Add to the pan with some butter and simmer for several minutes. Mix the eggs with salt and pepper. Pour the eggs in the pan and allow it to solidify. Add cheese if you wish to the top of the omelette and fold over. Cook for a further two minutes and serve.

Autumn

Autumn has to be my favourite season. There is something about the forest that seems to come alive, despite the fact the opposite is true as the trees begin to shed their leaves. Maybe it's the increase in the number of edible mushrooms or the first appearance of nuts and berries. In terms of sheer nutritional value, I would argue autumn is the best time of year for the Woodland Warrior.

As the days become shorter, the light of the full moon will be the only thing illuminating your way through the beech and oak trees.

Hazel (Corylus Avellana) September – October

The hazel is a shrubby tree commonly found in wood and hedgerows across Britain. Its key identifying features are the grey bark, yellow catkins, and the most precious commodity for the Woodland Warrior, the nuts.

The English name derives from the Anglo-Saxon *haesal* which translates to hat. One can only conclude this is in reference to its frilly cap in which the valued nut sits.

The use of this nut is truly prehistoric. They formed a crucial part of the Mesolithic hunter-gatherers diet. Pick a hazelnut and you are creating a direct link to your very first ancestors, and In common folklore the hazelnut tree is considered the tree of knowledge.

The nuts remain on the tree until ripe, falling off in the early autumn. The nut casing should be brown by this stage.

You will be in constant battle with the many birds and other mammals that also find this nut of great use. You will learn to loath the squirrel that has taken your stash of hazelnuts for the third consecutive time. The nuts can be stored in a cool dry place for up to several months.

Weight for weight, they have five times more protein than eggs. 20g of hazelnuts contain the following: 176 calories, 5g of protein, and 17g of fat.

Recipe – Campfire Roasted Hazelnuts

In my opinion, hazelnuts are abundant and taste delicious just as they are straight out of the shell, so any kind of processing may not be necessary. But if you fancy having a bit of fun with them while camping in the forest, try the following.

Ingredients: Hazelnuts (a quantity of your choice)

Method: Place the hazelnuts over an open fire in a cast iron pot or something similar. Roast for 10-15 minutes until you begin to hear the shells pop. Allow to cool before eating.

Hawthorn (Crataegus Monogyna) September – October

The hawthorn tree is easily one of the most common trees across the British Isles. Used frequently to create field boundaries, you're likely to be unable to walk more than a few steps outside your door before you encounter one. It has two crops that are valuable to the Woodland Warrior; the leaves in the spring and the berries in the autumn. Both contain the same benefits outlined below.

The hawthorn tree is quite easy to identify. In the spring, look for the leaves of both the common and mittel hawthorn, both of which are two edible species. It will also have a distinctive blossom of white flowers in the late spring. The red berries in the autumn will also stand out, but be aware of both white and black bryony, a plant that also has red berries (these are far brighter as well as spherical in appearance) and can sometimes infiltrate the hawthorn with its long vines.

The hawthorn tree is rich in folklore. It was once believed that it was unlucky to bring hawthorn into one's home, as it would likely result in the death of a loved one. A Glastonbury, there is a hawthorn tree that sprouted from the staff of Joseph of Arimathea. The tree grows to this very day, said to blossom without fail come Christmas. Pagans will bathe their faces with the dew of the hawthorn on May Day in the belief it enables them to be beautiful for an eternity.

Hawthorn is world renowned for its benefits to the cardiac system. The unique flavonoids within hawthorn relax the blood vessels within the main arteries, relieving blood pressure. Extended periods of consumption have well researched effects on all symptoms of heart disease. As one of the leading causes of death worldwide, a Woodland Warrior would be a fool not to use this elixir of life on a daily basis.

Some reports also suggest it is a mild sedative, helping to improve sleep quality and lower feelings of anxiety.

Recipe – Hawthorn Fruit Leather

You need to invest some time in collecting roughly one basket or half a bucket of hawthorn berries. It is also messy business, so best to mix it up outside. You will need a mixing bowl and some strong mesh material.

Ingredients: 500g Hawthorn Berries, water.

Method: Place the hawthorns in a bowl or bucket to mix. Try to make sure as many leaves and small stalks are removed. Initially add roughly one pint of water. Begin to crush with your hands until you have a glutinous paste which will be a mix of stones and berry flesh. Add more water if the mixture feels particularly dry, but not so much that you can visibly see excess liquid. Now put the mixture into some kind of strong mesh material. I use the same mesh bags as I would for foraging. Squeeze the mixture as hard as possible until the berry paste emerges. Spread flat over a non-stick clean baking tray and place in the oven on a low heat for up to two hours. This is also possible over a campsite fire; this is just the drying process, this drying option will take considerably longer than the oven. You should now have a dried 'fruit leather' which you can break up and take as an incredibly healthy post or pre-workout Woodland Warrior snack.

Common Puffball (Lycoperdon perlatum) September – November

Despite the fact I keep going on about autumn being the time of the mushroom, I am only including one fungus within this season. I've chosen to air on the side of caution, and I'm very confident the Puffball is incredibly difficult to get mixed up with any other poisonous mushrooms. With the increase in the number of mushrooms available, the possibility that you will pick something incorrectly also increases. Another reason is the fact that *Lycoperdon perlatum* is incredibly common in woodlands. I rarely enter a forest and don't find it in very large quantities.

The common puffball is saprotrophic, and consumes decaying organic matter, hence why it loves the woods in the autumn. It is also known as the pearl studded puffball, as sometimes it can appear to have small 'spikes' on its crown. Some fellow foragers don't consider it to be that tasty, but I find it has a light mushroom flavour with hints of the very forest in which it grows, almost as if its puffy flesh has taken on the scents and flavours of the forest purely through osmosis, like a sponge. All wild mushrooms share similar medicinal and nutritional benefits, regardless of their genus. This is a good place to start for any beginner and should encourage you to gain wider knowledge of all autumnal fungi. I believe this was the first wild mushroom I consumed as a young boy.

Its Latin name translates to 'wolfs flatulence'. How on earth it got that name we will never know. As this mushroom ages, the spores inside mature and are realised once the outer layer is broken, almost emitting a 'puff' like cloud of brown spores, so this is my best guess. If the flesh inside isn't completely white, then don't eat it. Avoid breathing in any of the spores as well. There are several types of puffball that are all similar in this regard and they are all edible. Avoid any that appear brown or dark in appearance. There is the common earth ball, but this is rock hard and has a solid purple centre. It isn't deadly poisonous, but it will give you incredibly bad stomach cramps. It's also possible to confuse puffballs with the egg like stage of the Amanita mushroom, so make sure you're familiar with the aforementioned. You may come across the giant puffball; this can become the size of football, and is unmistakable for any other mushroom, and it will provide you with ample edible flesh.

In terms of mushrooms, the puffball is surprisingly abundant in protein; 100g equates to 44g of protein. *Lycoperdon perlatum* is currently being studied for its highly unique antimicrobial properties and the fact that it contains the uncommon lycoperdic acid.

Recipe – Puffball Wolf Sauce

As with all the mushrooms, your easiest bet is to simply fry up and serve with whatever you wish. That being said, maybe you can impress the lady or gent of the woodland by serving your favourite pasta dish with this puffball based sauce. This recipe can be used for all the other mushrooms that have been recommended within this part of the programme. This also uses some of the other wild edibles listed in part five.

Ingredients: 500g of puffballs (or other mushrooms), 30g butter, 1 garlic clove, 125 ml of red wine or mead, 1 beef stock cube (or vegetarian), 3 yarrow leaves, 200ml cream.

Method: Heat the butter in the pan and add the chopped garlic clove for 2 minutes. Chop up the mushrooms and add those and season. After several minutes add the wine or mead, then add the yarrow leaves, plus the stock cube. Let the liquid reduce down by roughly two thirds, allow to cool, and then add the cream. Check the seasoning is to your tastes then serve.

Winter

And so we arrive at our last season. The tree branch from which you hang may even have a covering of frost or a few inches of snow.

Winter, particularly November and December, offers us some more fungi to fill our bellies, and one constant species of plant that refuses to disappear completely.

Wood Ear (Auricularia auricula-judae) September – February

The wood ear is a constant presence in the woodland. Technically I find it's at its most prevalent during the winter months, but it does appear all year round apart from high summer. Even when it disappears in the summer it has simply dried up to be $1/10^{th}$ of its size, you can still see small dark speckles on an elder tree, its preferred habitat. If you were to take it home and submerge it in water overnight, it would soon expand to its edible size. It is commonly used in Asian cooking in soups and stir fries but hasn't ever been a staple of the western diet.

It gets its Latin name from the myth that Judas of Iscariot hung himself from the elder tree. It is occasionally found on other host trees. Their texture is rubbery, and they do often look like an actual ear. They hold a strong place in Chinese folklore and traditional medicine as having both anti-aging and life extending qualities.

Nutritionally, they are a good source of energy at having 46g of carbohydrates per 100g. One test-tube study revealed that wood ear mushrooms inhibited the activity of beta secretase, an enzyme that releases beta amyloid proteins. Beta secretase is toxic to the brain and has been linked to degenerative diseases such as Alzheimer's.

Recipe – Wood Ear Tomato Soup

This is one of the few mushrooms that you can't just simply throw in the pan and fry as it will explode when exposed to high heats. The easiest way to consume this mushroom is to simply chop into small slices and then gently heat for a few minutes on the hob along with your soup of choice. I personally find it goes well with tomato soup, hence this recipe. I don't promise that this mushroom will be to everyone's liking, particularly if you don't like slippery textures.

Ingredients: 10 wood ear mushrooms, 1 can of tomatoes, 1 onion, and 30g butter.

Method: Melt the butter in a sauce pan; add the diced onion, and tomatoes. Add water and leave to simmer for 40 minutes and reduce to the desired consistency. Cool and then blend. Chop up your wood ear mushrooms into thin slices. Add the now blended soup back into a sauce pan with the wood ear mushrooms, heat gently for 4-5 minutes. Season with salt and pepper.

Wood Blewits (Lepista *Nuda) November – January*

When you come across a mushroom on the woodland floor that isn't simply monotone and instead has a bright purple sheen, it does take on a certain magical quality. The lilac tops and stems of the Wood Blewit peak above the fallen leaves and logs of the forest floor like no other mushroom. It has a certain quality that sends one's mind back to a by gone age, when the local workers of the land would pick up their basket and venture in a woodland not yet disturbed by widespread deforestation.

They are quite unusual to eat, typical mushroom flavour with an almost floral hint and a touch of orange. Nothing else within the mushroom kingdom really compares. They also have an unusual texture; sticky and slimy, but don't let this put you off as it certainly isn't excessive.

Wood blewits must be cooked otherwise they will cause gastric upset. In sensitive individuals, this still may be the case even after cooking, so do take some care. They have a preference for woods with a higher number of beech trees. 'Blewit' is a corruption of 'blue hat'.

There isn't a great deal you could confuse them with. *Laccaria amethystine* is also a deep shade of purple, but these are not poisonous. Some form of webcap mushrooms however are, so please take care and perform further research on both.

Wood blewits tend to grow in rings. Much folklore surrounds these rings in all European cultures. Some believe the rings represented the areas of the woods where fairies and elves would meet to perform magical rituals and to dance under a full moon. They may have also acted as a portal between the real world and that of the mythical creatures of the woodland. This circle is actually caused by how the mycelium network underground chooses to grow, the mushroom just being a representation of its fruiting body and way to procreate.

Nutritionally wood blewits once again share the common benefits of mushrooms. Blewits are particularly high in thiamine. This micronutrient helps considerably with digesting food and converting it into energy ready for your next workout.

Recipe – Blewits on toast

Blewits can be treated like any other mushroom, but just make sure they are cooked thoroughly. This simple blewit on toast recipe should mean you have no excuse but to tap into this magical woodland ingredient.

Ingredients: Some thick cut country bread, 4 blewits, butter and/or vegetable oil

Methods: Heat some oil in the pan and add some nice thick cut country bread. A couple of minutes each side will make it crispy and delicious. Chop up the blewits, and then add to a separate pan with some vegetable oil or butter. Season with salt and pepper, and then cook until soft. Serve on top of the toasted bread and enjoy.

Goosegrass (Galium Aparine) February – May

Goosegrass is unmistakable. Otherwise known as sticky weed or cleavers, it's the plant you threw at your mate walking home from school, so it would stick on his blazer or jumper. Its Velcro-like stems and petal star shaped flowers can't even be missed by the most ill-sighted of foragers.

A plant that can pretty much be found in varying quantities throughout the year, from the sides of paths to the edges of woodlands, you won't ever have any trouble finding goosegrass. It will be less visible in high summer and winter. It grows in dense bundles, and often overcomes the hedges of its chosen habitat. It's possible to create small parcels and steam or boil them like any other green vegetable, but I would be lying if I said I ever found this especially appetising. Goosegrass is related to the coffee plant and contains modest amounts of caffeine. It was extensively used in medieval kitchens due to its ability to survive snow and frost. The 17th century herbalist John Gerard would recommend a cleavers tonic to assist women with weight loss. It probably had this effect due to the diuretic properties of caffeine. The plant is also high in vitamin C, a trait it shares with many common plants.

Recipe – Woodland Warrior Winter Tonic

Utilise this drink during your Woodland Warrior workouts to get a little bit of an extra kick from the caffeine and help keep your immune system strong during the colder winter months. It tastes mostly of cucumber.

Ingredients: Goosegrass, water.

Method: Grab a handful of goosegrass and create a small parcel by simply bunching up in your hand. Add to a large jug or sealed bottle and fill with water. Leave in the fridge overnight to infuse. Feel free to add lemon, or other wild edible plants for a greater infusion and taste.

Conclusion

And so we come to the end of our seasonal guide to the wild edibles recommended for the Woodland Warrior. As stated previously, these choices are simply the tip of the iceberg; hundreds of wild edibles await your discovery through further research and experience. I hope these small choices encourage you to explore nature's larder as much as possible. Remember to only take what you need. I have no doubt regular consumption of these plants and fungi will have a noticeable effect upon your overall health and performance.

"The naturalist is a civilised hunter. He goes alone into the field or woodland and closes his mind to everything but that time and place, so that life around him presses in on all the senses and small details grow in significance" E.O Wilson

There aren't many things in this world I can imagine that are better than camping outdoors in woodland regardless of the season.

That search for firewood, food, and the perfect branch. The freedom of simply packing a bag, throwing your tent over your shoulder and choosing one of the many stunning wild camping sites or whatever form of wilderness takes your fancy.

This part of the programme will touch upon the very basics of wild camping; I am not a miniature version of Ray Mears, and this will simply be some of the very foundational aspects of camping I've picked up over the years. Hundreds of books exist by very talented authors that go into an amazing amount of detail on both camping and the survival methods of bushcraft. These should make for essential reading. Camping isn't for everyone; it can be far removed from modern comforts. But the Woodland Warrior should seek and become accustomed to feeling uncomfortable.

Within us all, the primal urge to sleep under the stars exists. Not long ago, 'camping' was the daily existence for many human beings.

What should you take?

I always recommend travelling light; only take the absolute essentials with you. When it comes to cost of equipment, buy whatever you can afford. If you intend to go wild camping regularly then it may be beneficial to purchase higher quality equipment. If you're on a budget eBay can often prove to be a good place to start.

You ideally want a backpack that is at least 60 litres in capacity. If you plan on travelling long distances or hiking, then a mixture of comfort and practicality for your own individual needs is paramount.

If you are a casual camper, it is best to stay away from makeshift shelters, tarps, and bivvy bags for the time being. You're going to want a decent lightweight tent. I've personally always used Vango tents, and I find them to be a high-quality brand. Avoid a one-man tent, as I often find them far too small and the makers clearly had a hobbit in mind during their design. Which can be fine if you actually are one. Two man or above should work well, and go for three if you're expecting a visitor. I hear the Dryads can be a bit saucy.

Most of all make sure that whatever tent you buy is proven to be water proof. I've spent many a soggy night due to this mistake. You aren't going to feel like you've stayed in a 5 star hotel, but you will get used to it and even grow to like it.

When it comes to a sleeping bag, you are going to want something that will be great for all three seasons. You can either go for a traditional mummy bag, or the envelope style. I like to move around quite a bit and I don't like to feel like a moth that's about to emerge from a cocoon, so the envelope is always my choice. I like to put all my clothing for the next day in the bag with me before I go to sleep for extra warmth (if needs be, I won't bother in the summer) and with some practice it's possible to get dressed in your sleeping bag. Make sure you have a water proof bag to carry it in. Snugpack normally make decent sleeping bags suitable for all seasons. I suggest you take extra woollen blankets with you for the winter months.

Taking a small one ring stove is essential, regardless of whether you intend to start a fire or not. You will be shocked that despite the fact you have watched 19 YouTube videos on how to start a fire, it's still can be incredibly hard to do, especially in challenging conditions. Remember a small gas canister, and have an extra one just in case, especially if you intend the trip to last more than a few nights. When it comes to cutlery and cooking materials, plenty of multi-tools exist, this also applies to pots and pans. Research lightweight options that can double up as a pan, plate, or pot. A basic first aid kit is essential along with some water purification tablets just in case. Resist the urge to try and look like Rambo with a giant machete, and invest in a decent pocketknife.

Other near essentials may include a fire lighting kit, which could simply be basic kindling like newspaper and matches. Learning how to use natural tinder and mastering natural fire lighting methods are a good investment once you've gained more outdoor experience. A head torch, and some spare batteries is always a good idea. An axe is beneficial if you intend to chop wood either for a workout or to make a campfire. You may possibly need a compass and a map if you want to be old school and really wander off into the wilderness, but I guess modern smart phones now make these a little bit redundant unless you are stranded somewhere with no signal. I won't patronise you further and make a long list of suitable clothing for that particular season. If you choose to run around the woods in the middle of January with nothing but your vest on, expect to get cold. Layers are always superior to one thick layer. Depending on the extent of just how wild your camping will be, you may or may not be able to have a shower, so keep this in mind and please take care if you want to venture into any ponds, you may actually come out more filthy than when you entered.

Being prepared

This doesn't just apply to camping, but I've always admired the following motto: fail to prepare, prepare to fail. It really has served me well throughout my life. I can't remember where I've stolen it from, probably the scouts.

There will be times when challenges present themselves. You may suffer a cut from a swing of your axe and the first aid kit you remembered to pack now becomes essential. Organisation will allow you to enjoy your trip more knowing you're prepared for all scenarios.

Weather is unpredictable. Have a waterproof set of clothing, both bottom and top, ready to slip on when necessary. Practise putting your tent up prior to your trip, in both good and bad weather conditions, and potentially time yourself to try to get this down to a matter of minutes. If you and your equipment are wet, you will suffer. The ability to put your tent up quickly could make all the difference.

Research well before hand the area in which you intend to camp, and unless you're in Scotland, probably best not to anger Farmer Jones by camping in the middle of his dairy paddock. Wild camping does have a greater level of freedom in Scotland compared to the rest of Britain, but I would say many campsites exist that can put you in the centre of a woodland or on the edge of a coastal cliff. Always check the weather forecast, but if you're in the UK you know full well we can sometimes have all four seasons in a matter of hours. Wherever you choose, be smart, select somewhere that appears relatively dry and is preferably flat. Check the surrounding canopy in the woodland and ensure it looks likely you won't experience any branches falling on top of your tent if weather conditions turn sour. And no matter how deserted the beach, remember the tide always arrives. This may affect what you should wear and where you will travel. I always keep any food I take with me near the top of my rucksack so I can quite easily grab a snack on the go if I begin to feel my energy levels start to drop. When it comes to insects, I don't see them as a considerable threat in Britain. If you're heading to areas with built up vegetation, which can come with woodland territories and high populations of deer, then tics may present a problem. Always check your whole body for tics and have a tic comb ready. Keeping your camping area tidy always helps with organisation. You want to be able to find whatever you require as quickly as possible in some scenarios.

Fire

If you bring a stove, a fire isn't absolutely essential, but done correctly it does have a certain wild quality to it. You're completing a behaviour that dates back to the very start of our evolutionary history. Make sure you have the landowner's permission (or the campsite owner's) before lighting any kind of fire. Being in close proximity to a wood will make lighting and maintaining a fire far easier. A fire will always need three things: air, heat and fuel. Fire preparation isn't as easy as it first appears and will take some practise.

Find a nice flat piece of ground, avoiding as much vegetation as possible. Use rocks to create a fire bed that surrounds it so it can't spread beyond its perimeter. Lay a bed of dry sticks for the fire floor, ensuring these sticks are as dry as possible. Tinder is essential. Birch bark shavings are a great choice because they contain natural oils that burn well. There is also a fungus called 'King Alfred's Cakes' which look like large lumps of charcoal. They can be found abundantly all year round on various types of trees and are a good way to transport a fire because they hold and generate heat well. They are named after King Alfred due to the legend that while on the run from the Vikings, King Alfred took shelter in a peasant women's home. She asked him to watch over some cakes she was baking in her absence, but he ended up burning them and being scolded by the woman. You will need some kindling to help create a proper fire when larger logs are added. Avoid any twigs that are green or do not appear fully dry. Pile the kindling in a wigwam shape to maximise air flow. Once you can see clear flames, gradually add logs.

Food

When it comes to food, there is a lot of personal preference. Hopefully you are able to find some if not all of the wild edibles I've described earlier on in this book during your camping trip. Wild foods that are dense in energy are a rarity, but one prolific example that I did not mentioned earlier is Burdock Root, which has a root that if cooked, is slightly reminiscent of parsnip. So this is a backup if you've forgotten your bag of pasta. Your best bet is to take non-perishable and calorie dense foods, such as nuts, dried fruit, oat based snack bars, small packages of porridge, and a few whole-wheat based peanut butter sandwiches. If you are nearer to civilisation and can acquire sources of fresh products, remember to only buy foods that you can cook in a pot over your stove. Don't forget coffee if you're a caffeine addict like me. Dandelion root coffee doesn't really cut it in my experience, despite the medicinal benefit. Wild Camping can be an energy demanding activity so keep this in mind; it's always good to keep a few extra supplies in your mode of transport if need be.

Water

You can live up to three weeks without food but only three days without water, so this just exemplifies how much of a necessity it is. Wild Camping sites are legally obliged to provide safe drinking water, but if you've wondered off into absolute wilderness, this may prove more challenging. Try to consume at least two litres a day; the most basic way to do this is to ensure you take two litre bottles with you. The key to obtaining natural drinking water is identifying a good source. Try to choose a flowing river; you should at least double treat your water to ensure its safe to drink. Some methods of purification include boiling, filtering through a sock, or buying a charcoal filter. Water purification tablets make your life a lot easier. Boiling the water first, then pulling the sock over the top of your chosen container should remove most impurities. Remember to allow the water to cool prior to putting it into any kind of plastic bottle. The water purification tablets take 30 minutes, but I believe it is still a good idea to filter through a sock or a similar material. Be aware of the area and what sort of farming practices may occur close by if you decide to choose a natural water source. Keep in mind that despite all your best efforts the water may not still not be entirely pure, practice and understand fully techniques for water purification before consuming the end result.

Wild camping in winter

Winter camping does add both its unique challenges and unique benefits. I don't recommend that your very first camping trip is in the middle of January during one of the rare times we experience snow. But I do believe eventually it's beneficial for both experience and practical awareness to try camping during all months. Always ensure your gear is up to the task of harsher conditions and realise that lighting a fire may be twice as challenging.

Winter camping will offer you even more solitude if that's what you are seeking. Only the truly hardy will venture out in such conditions. And the scenery can be even more striking than during the summer; the forest floor may be littered with deep shades of purple, fluorescent yellows, and golden brown caps of numerous different fungi.

Why wild camping?

I hope this programme has already adequately explained why any kind of immersion in nature is nothing but a good thing. Wild Camping allows you to switch off from the mainstream world, even if it's only just for a few nights. Disconnecting regularly for long periods of time is miraculous for one's own physical and mental well-being in this often contact saturated world we now live in. You will be surprised how much you may enjoy your own company from time to time.

The wilderness tends to the wild nature we all have innately entwined within our souls. It feeds the Mesolithic beasts we once were. The wild is the beast maker. There is often a fear that needs to be overcome when it comes to wild camping. But once you free yourselves from the shackles of modernity and all its comforts, even just for the briefest of moments, you will know what it is to be alive once again.

Part 7 – Exercise Demonstrations plus Plant and Fungi Identification

I hope you will now be able to walk into any woodland and see before you not just an ensemble of different trees, but a place where muscle can be built and well-being increased.

I want you to know how it feels to hang from a branch with the texture of bark under your knuckles. I want you to know what it's like to see not leaf litter, but the intricate patterns of different fungi that lurk on the forest floor. Most importantly, I want you to have a new infinity with nature, an acceptance that we are not separate from it but a part of it.

You now know a method which will allow you to build muscle, increase strength, and utilise your nutrition all simply from an environment that has existed since nearly the dawn of time. Go forth and become a warrior that any woodland would be proud to claim as their own.

Please find photos of exercise demonstrations and plant identification in this part of the programme. These are not necessarily in the order in which they appear in the text. I will also provide exercise demonstrations for The Woodland Warrior on my campsite YouTube channel in the near future. As this is the 2nd edition, you may well see a difference in my physique with the new photos taken in the year since the start of the pandemic (The pull-up, log tricep dip, and log inverted row photos remain from the 1st edition). Spending a far greater time outdoors and eating more wild foraged foods has meant I've noticed some considerable changes. I hope you witness the same effect on your own body. If you're wondering why I have no footwear on in some photos, I was practicing grounding. Something I will elaborate more on in a future title.

I advocate you giving the workouts as much effort as you can, but I also hope you find them a lot of fun!

You can also send any feedback or questions to the Dagger Wood Campsite Instagram page or its email address.

Instagram: https://www.instagram.com/daggerwood_campsite/

Email: *daggercamping@gmail.com*

Common Puffball
(*Lycoperdon perlatum*)

The Field Mushroom
(*Agaricus campestris*)

Wood Blewit (*Lepista nuda*)

Wood Ear (*Auricularia auricula-judae*)

Kind Alfred's Cakes (*Daldinia concentrica*) – as mentioned in part 6

Stinging Nettle (Urtica *Dioica*)

Hawthorn (Crataegus *monogyna*) in bloom during the spring

Garlic Mustard (Alliaria *petiolate*)

Yarrow (Achillea *millefolium*)

Dryads Saddle (*Polyporus squamosus*)

Common Sorrel
(Rumex *acetosa*)

Goosegrass (Galium *aparine*)

Log Crucifix Hold

Tree Pull-ups

Log Overhead-Press

Log Land-Mine Press

Log Good-Mornings

Log Over-Head Tricep Extensions

Log Land-Mine Row

Log Tricep Dips

Log Inverted-Rows

Log Deadlift

Log Bent Over Row

Log Shrugs

Log Front Squats

An example of the rope handles used for all logs.

This is just a simple double knot. Make sure the length of rope fits around the entire log.

If the rope proves too long for the specific exercise, just loop it around your fist until it's the appropriate length.

Printed in Great Britain
by Amazon

22125972R00057